The Rabbit Hole Experience

Praise for The Rabbit Hole Experience

These guys are talking about something important that doesn't get much attention because it only resonates loudly with witnesses and squatchers who really do get action in the field. I know I honestly like a Bigfoot research book if it's making me want to look at maps of the area.

— **Matt Moneymaker**
Founder, Bigfoot Field
Researchers Organization

The Rabbit Hole Experience is a dialogue that should be attended by both believers and skeptics: How do we develop a language potent enough to capture the full range of the uncanny? Paul and Michael grapple with the very human experiences of those who've confronted something-that-cannot-be-and-yet-seems-to-be.

— **Joshua Blu-Buhs**
Bigfoot: The Life
and Times of a Legend

Few books eloquently explore what happens to those who experience the unexplainable. This one does. Robartes and Conroy reveal the human experience with the otherworldly through real case studies. One doesn't have to believe in the super-natural to appreciate how *The Rabbit Hole Experience* unveils the transformative experience of wonderment.

— **Deonna Kelli Sayed**
Paranormal Obsession: America's Fascination with Ghosts & Hauntings, Spooks & Spirits and *So You Want To Hunt Ghosts? A Down-To-Earth Guide*

You will delight in joining this investigation for you shall live, up close and personal, the chills and excitement these folks have deeply felt in the woods and other byways they have explored. Too often, books sharing the paranormal points of view of Sasquatch hunting hold the readers at arm's length. That is certainly not true of this text. Come along on the authors' journey down *The Rabbit Hole Experience*!

— **Loren Coleman**
Director, International
Cryptozoology Museum
Portland, Maine

In my twenty-five plus years of writing about things that cannot be explained, I have yet to experience the presence of a ghost, see a UFO, or witness a Bigfoot. If I did, I would imagine it would have a profound psychological impact on my beliefs. In *The Rabbit Hole Experience*, Paul and Michael have entered that dark area of un-reality. They make sense of true-life encounters with something that is not understood. Many of these experiences took place in the New Jersey/New York area, which makes the tone of the book even more frightening and … weird!

— **Mark Sceurman**
Co-publisher, *Weird NJ Magazine*

The Rabbit Hole Experience

On Sasquatches, Spirits, and the People Who See Them

Paul Conroy & Michael Robartes

Foreword by L'Aura Hladık Hoffman

CΔPE
HOUSE
CAPE HOUSE BOOKS
ALLENDALE, NEW JERSEY

THE RABBIT HOLE EXPERIENCE
On Sasquatches, Spirits, and the People Who See Them

Cape House Books™
PO Box 200
Allendale, NJ 07401-0200
www.CapeHouseBooks.com

Cover and book design by Bill Ash

Cataloging-in Publication Data

Conroy, Paul and Michael Robartes
The Rabbit Hole Experience: On Sasquatches, Spirits, and the
People Who See Them / Paul Conroy and Michael Robartes ;
Foreword by L'Aura Hladik Hoffman

p. cm.

ISBN 978-1-939129-12-3

1. Parapsychology 2. Spirit phenomena 3.Paranormal-sightings
4.Paranormal-investigations 5. Sightings-interviews

I. Title   II. Authors

Includes bibliographical references.

P322 C55 2018   130 CO

180715

Dedications

For my good friend Bob Canino, a true seeker who moved forward on his journey before he could see this book manifest.

—Michael Robartes

For the courageous witnesses whose stories live between these pages.

—Paul Conroy

"Why, sometimes I've believed as many as six impossible things before breakfast."

—Lewis Carroll, *Alice in Wonderland*

Contents

Foreword

IN my twenty-five years of paranormal investigating, aka ghost hunting, I've never heard or used the term "Rabbit Hole Experience." But after reading this book, I confidently say it has a rightful place on the vocabulary list for this field of study.

The Rabbit Hole Experience truly defines the essence of that moment one finds themselves in the midst of an occurrence that supersedes all they know and accept as "normal."

Authors Paul Conroy and Michael Robartes have worked many years in their fields — Sasquatch and paranormal investigating, respectively — and helped many people confronted with the paranormal. In this book the two investigators shine the light of cognitive dissonance psychology on their clients' encounters.

This psychological component, combined with their varied experiences, makes *The Rabbit Hole Experience* a compelling and enlightening read.

The Rabbit Hole Experience

Each chapter brings the reader into a story from both authors' perspectives. This approach creates the feeling of telling ghost stories around the campfire. It's easy to follow along even if you don't use paranormal investigation tech.

Whether you feared a monster under your bed as a child or do the nightly "monster check" for your children now, this book is hard to put down. One minute you'll feel comforted with an explanation so deftly presented. The next, you'll be second-guessing every creak you hear in your own home.

For paranormal investigators, this book is a must-read. Sure, you think you know all there is to know because you've been ghost hunting for a couple of years. You have all the latest gadgets and equipment and aren't afraid to use them. But you may be like a surgeon with a state-of-the-art operating room and years of surgical finesse but no bedside manner.

The Rabbit Hole Experience is the owner's manual for compassionately navigating the fear, confusion, and shock witnesses feel after their paranormal encounter. It's simple: Knowledge is power. Understanding how an individual processes an event allows an investigator to get more details—and possibly tangible evidence—during a subsequent investigation.

If you are brand new to paranormal investigating, I recommend this book. Believe me, you'll amass a library of books on the subject. I have shelves filled with titles by Hans Holzer, Ed and Lorraine Warren, Brad Steiger, Jeff Belanger, Arthur Myers, and Rosemary Ellen Guiley.

Television shows are not the best study guides for working as a paranormal investigator. You have to put in the time reading all the books written by those I previously mentioned: they ghost hunted long before it was cool to be on television.

When I started in 1993, Jeff, my then-husband, and I dined at haunted restaurants, pretending to celebrate our anniversary but covertly photographing. We also took the long way to and from the restrooms with our analog audio recorders in our pockets, hoping to capture an EVP (Electronic Voice Phenomena). We chose haunted hotels and bed and breakfasts for our weekend getaways and vacations.

Back then, we couldn't admit to paranormal investigating because the reactions of people around us were more frightening than the ghosts.

After one pseudo-anniversary dinner at the General Wayne Inn outside Philadelphia, I closed the swinging doors of a bathroom stall in the ladies' room with an eyehook latch. I did this perfectly and hung my purse on a hook on the stall wall. Once finished, I reached for my purse and the swinging doors, which were unlatched, opened slightly. I stared at the eyehook dangling perpendicular to the floor. I had latched it perfectly, parallel to the floor. A chill like no other swept through me. I exited quickly.

I ran to the bar and told Jeff about the door unlocking itself. The bartender/restaurant manager overheard me.

"You just met our pervert ghost," he said in his delightful brogue. "He either resides in the ladies' room or here by the bar. He likes to pinch the ladies seated at the bar and watch as they smack the poor fella who is near them."

We confided in him that we'd come specifically for the ghosts. Thrilled, he took us on a tour of the entire restaurant, pointing out all the places he and others had had encounters.

I had my Rabbit Hole Experience that night, but I didn't have a name for it—until now. Since then, I've had more: A ghost walked through me. An unseen hand turned my digital audio recorder forty-five degrees while it lay on a kitchen counter.

Now it's your turn.

— L'Aura Hladik Hoffman
Founder/Director,
New Jersey Ghost Hunters Society
Author, *Ghosthunting New Jersey*, *Ghosthunting New York City*, and *Ghosts of the Poconos*

Preface

WE explore worlds that most people believe to be fiction. In more than a decade of investigating reports of Sasquatch and spirit activity, we've spent many hours around campfires, holed up in tents in the rain or standing in swamps in the dead of winter or heat of summer.

All that time, we've compared notes, paying particular attention to the reactions of witnesses to their experiences.

Gradually, we saw commonalities among the witnesses in the aftermath of their encounters with the unknown. There was something more fundamental at work that transcended the differences in the details. Their initial experience was frightening, but their reactions didn't stop there. In many cases, they lived in a state akin to post-traumatic stress disorder. What they saw fundamentally shattered their belief structure about what is real and possible, leaving them in some cases with nothing to grasp onto.

The Rabbit Hole Experience

This is the phenomenon we refer to as the Rabbit Hole Experience (RHE). It is a part of the paranormal story you don't see on TV. It's seen only by those working in the trenches in the various fields of paranormal investigation.

In these pages we share our experiences, thoughts, and theories on this phenomenon. We hope our research sheds light on this overlooked aspect of our work and inspires thoughtfulness about the effects these experiences have on witnesses.

This book is more about posing questions than providing answers. We discuss our own field notes and ideas framed in terms that we know. Our goals are to make sense of our own experiences while helping others who have nowhere else to turn.

Although the word "paranormal" has come to be used almost synonymously with ghosts, we use the term in its broadest sense to refer to any experience outside what most people consider normal. It does not imply anything necessarily supernatural. Bigfoots, ghosts, UFOs and many other experiences will be classified under the broad heading of paranormal. When we wish to discuss things specific to one area or another, we will specify further.

We have changed names and locations to protect the anonymity of our clients and witnesses, but everything else is reported exactly as we experienced it or as related to us by witnesses.

Preface

We've written in a conversational style that lets each of us speak in his own voice. We hope this approach conveys the feeling of the reader sitting with us in one of the fireside conversations during which these ideas took shape.

Paul Conroy and Michael Robartes

The Rabbit Hole Experience

I. The Candle Incident

PAUL: In July 2012 Michael and I were weary and mosquito-bitten but very excited as we returned to his cabin from four days of fieldwork in the swamps of St. Lawrence County, New York. We had developed a rapport with two witnesses who were experiencing potential Sasquatch activity. They lived within two miles of each other along the St. Lawrence River that divides New York from Canada. Each was unaware of the other's experience.

The history of reports in this region dates back to 1604 when French explorer Samuel de Champlain explored the St. Lawrence River. (He lends his name to Lake Champlain and even to Champ, the lake monster supposedly in it. I should be so lucky.) He recorded in his journals stories of a giant, hairy humanoid creature the local Indian tribes called "Gougou."[1]

---

[1] See Paul Bartholomew, et al., *Monsters of the Northwoods*

We had interesting experiences to discuss, audio to analyze, and a lot of general information to process. We were looking forward to replacing some of the calories we'd lost in the field with several Amy's® frozen pizzas while sorting out all that we had taken in over the last ninety-six hours.

As we entered the cabin, Michael matter-of-factly noted that a candle on the woodstove was burning. It took me a few seconds to wrap my mind around the point he was trying to make. We had just walked in the door. He hadn't lit it. It wasn't the fact it was burning. It was the fact it was *still* burning.

I have been an investigator with the Bigfoot Field Researchers Organization (BFRO) since 2005. I met Michael on the 2006 BFRO expedition in Whitehall, New York, but it wasn't until afterwards that we struck up direct conversation. Initially, the two of us seemed to float in a unique boat when compared to some of the other attendees. We agreed the stories of others were impressive, and we both were well aware of the circumstantial evidence that exists within the Sasquatch community—casts, unclassified hair, footage that is interesting yet inconclusive. But we needed more before we declared a belief.

(Utica, NY: North Country Books, 1992), 2-3; Robert E. Bartholomew and Paul B. Bartholomew, *Bigfoot Encounters in New York and New England: Documented Evidence, Stranger than Fiction* (Blaine, WA: Hancock House, 2008), 18-19.

The Candle Incident

Mike accompanied me on my first solo overnight expedition. As the years went by, our friendship maintained and grew after we discovered we shared other interests. Over the years, as Michael invested more time in spirit research, we continued getting together for trips to the woods to look for monsters and share notes on our respective investigations. We were interested to find out how much our paths had in common.

But there also are some differences in our fields. A significant one is the dividing line between ourselves and the subjects we pursue. Conducting field research and investigating Sasquatch reports is indeed a risky business, particularly considering that much of our fieldwork is done at night. Whether we are crossing dilapidated wooden bridges over frigid mountain streams in wintertime, stumbling in the dark in the heart of bear country, or sharing the woods with hunters in the middle of spring turkey season, there are risks. But once we emerge from the forest, we are finished. The remote areas where we investigate alleged Sasquatch sightings act as a buffer zone between us and the subjects that we seek. While we sometimes experience "being followed" on our way out of forests as we return to the jeep, once we are on the road, the game is over.

Not so with Mike's work as it relates to potential spirit activity. We often had discussed the possibility of him taking his work home with him, a matter in which he may have no say. But I had never had a firsthand experience of anything that remotely resembled ghostly activity. Not until I stood staring at that candle.

Michael: I remember the look on Paul's face as he stood looking at the candle and his mind processed the data. I had seen that look on the faces of clients and members of my team, and they had similar reactions to Paul's: "What the fuck?" For me, this was nothing new. Sometimes objects move on their own. Sometimes voices speak without anyone there to utter the words. Sometimes candles light themselves. This is the world I live in.

I manage a paranormal investigation team called Scientific Paranormal (SP). It's affiliated with The Atlantic Paranormal Society (TAPS), the team behind the *Ghost Hunters* TV show. The TAPS Family teams do the work in the trenches, the work outside TV. If you contact TAPS with a case in our area, which covers a large part of New York State and occasionally spills over state lines, we will get the report and call to help you out.

As one who spends his nights intentionally prowling around haunted locations, I am often asked whether anything ever follows me home from an investigation. There are spirits around us all the time and activity in my house is not uncommon. It comes with the job. So when activity is occurring, it's hard to say whether it has anything to do with an investigation or whether it's just the locals. Still, it does happen from time to time. That's the nature of the endeavor. While no hairy primate, besides Paul, has ever followed me home from the woods, I do occasionally have hitchhikers from ghost investigations. Sometimes, spirits at a location will seize the opportunity of someone paying attention to them and follow investigators home in hopes of communicating.

Unfortunately for these spirits, I am not very sensitive. On one occasion, a spirit who apparently had followed me from a case got frustrated and followed a friend of mine home after she and I met for dinner. She reported that shortly after she got home that night, she suddenly felt exhausted and collapsed on her bed. As she lay there, unable to move, she heard the voice of a young girl talking to her. It sounded very similar to voices I had captured at the investigation. Apparently this spirit was frustrated at trying to get through to me and moved on to someone more receptive. Such are the perils of being friends with a ghost hunter.

So the possibility that one of these spirits felt the need to resort to lighting fires in order to get my attention was not inconceivable to me. But first we had to consider the more mundane possible explanations. This is the way we work. Even in a location that has legitimate paranormal activity, not everything that happens is paranormal. One of the most difficult but important parts of our job as investigators is separating what may be paranormal from what probably is not.

Paul: At the risk of speaking for both of us, I often do. Going in, we look for the obvious and rational explanation first. If Mike is contacted by a client who claims to hear loud banging in her walls and is certain that the ghost of Fortunato is desperately trying to escape, and there is a direct correlation between her first experience and the first chilly night of September, Mike may ask her to turn off her heat, wait a while, and turn it back on again. If Mike suddenly hears old Fortunato banging away, he feels quite confident that what his client hears is the percussive sound of heating ducts, and that old Fortunato remains sleeping peacefully.

Likewise for the witness who has contacted me after hearing strange vocalizations from the woods behind his house. We default to owl or coyote before jumping to hairy, yet-to-be-discovered monster.

So, facing this mystery of the candle, we did not want to jump to conclusions. We took a step back and considered the possibilities.

Four days prior, I had driven up to Mike's cabin in Central New York. We spent the night as is customary for us: we had dinner, loaded up Mike's jeep with our gear, and then settled down to discuss strategy as well as all things new in our respec-

The Candle Incident

tive fields of pursuit. We then got some sleep before setting out the next morning.

Mike was adamant he had blown out the candle before we had turned in. Considering I had slept eight feet from it and find it extremely difficult to fall asleep without complete darkness, I am sure he's right. There'd be no way I could've drifted off to sleep without getting up and blowing out the candle.

Michael: To put things in context, I don't own a TV or have Internet at my house. While I have electricity, it has always been my habit to light my house with candles and oil lamps once the sun goes down. Once all of these are blown out, the house is dark. It would be very difficult to fail to notice that a candle was still burning.

Paul: Even if we considered the remote possibility that we'd somehow left it burning all night, the candle was sitting atop Mike's Jøtul® woodstove, which is only a few feet from the door to the garage—a door that we would have entered and exited several times the following morning traveling from the cabin to the jeep as we loaded our gear and prepared to leave for the expedition. There is no way we would have passed by that candle multiple times the morning we left and not blown it out. We passed within three feet of it.

Living in a cabin, one becomes understandably maniacal when it comes to the ritual of extinguishing open flame before leaving—a ritual both of us are quite familiar with. My obsessive-compulsive disorder demands I shut off lights, confirm the stove is off, and check that the fireplace is well contained. Mike is the same way. You don't live in a house of logs while disrespecting fire.

Furthermore, even if we had left it burning, there was no way a candle that stood a mere few inches high by a couple of inches wide would continue to burn after four days. Even if it were large enough to sustain a flame for that long, it would have been burned down significantly, with wax that had liquefied and then hardened underneath as evidence. But there was none.

Coincidentally, my wife had worked for a large candle manufacturer only three years earlier. I decided to get some expert testimony. I called her from the cabin and relayed the details of our experience, asking her if it would be remotely possible for a candle four inches high by two-and-a-half inches wide to burn for more than eighty hours and continue burning with very little wax liquefied as a result. Her answer was simple: "No."

Michael: The possibility I considered was that the candle flame had burned so low at night that we did not notice it. Perhaps when I blew it out, the wick did not extinguish fully. Suppose it was barely an ember and burned like that for four days. Maybe our opening the door when we entered fed it enough oxygen to make the flame light up again. It was burning brightly when we saw it. This seemed to me to be the only natural possibility. The problem with the theory was that there was an open window about ten feet from the woodstove the whole time we were gone. There was certainly no lack of oxygen available for the flame. So it's difficult to imagine how this could have worked. Either the breeze from the window would have blown it out, or made it burn brighter and burn out long before we returned home.

Paul: Judging by the size of the candle and the lack of wax, we came to the conclusion it had only been burning for a few hours at the most.

So Mike and I discussed the next possibility: someone had come to Mike's cabin, unannounced, and felt the need to light a candle for us and do nothing more. But Mike's cabin is in a rural area and, at that point, he had lived there only one month. He had not yet met anyone from the neighborhood. There certainly would be no reason for any of them to enter the cabin, uninvited and unannounced, without good reason. They also had no knowledge regarding the fact he would be away for a significant length of time.

The Rabbit Hole Experience

Michael: I live alone, and at this time, even my beloved cat, Tinne, was not at the house. She was staying with my family, an hour-and-a-half's drive away, until I got fully moved into the new house. No one had any idea I was away, and even if they did, they would not know when we were coming back. Paul and I did not know when we would return. It depended on how things went up in St. Lawrence. So if someone wanted me to find a lit candle when I came home, he or she would have to guess pretty well on the timing of lighting it. Someone would be going pretty far out of his or her way with very little chance of timing it so we even saw the candle while it was lit.

Paul: When we considered the possibility of someone playing a joke, the subtlety of their actions confounded us. Hell, rearrange the furniture, involve mannequins or scarecrows, or toilet paper the trees, for God's sake.

So we came to the conclusion we almost certainly had not forgotten to blow out the candle. Even if we did, it could not have burned for all that time. Nor did we think someone went to Mike's cabin, broke in, and left everything undisturbed save for lighting a small candle.

As we settled down for the evening with the candle still burning (we didn't want to appear ungrateful), we discussed other possibilities. We were well trained in not letting mystery dilute rational thought as we considered as many conceivable scenarios as possible.

I was in mid-sentence when I heard the unmistakable sound of Mike's screen door opening, and then the gentle bang as it shut, a sound so recognizable that you could play me the audio with my eyes closed and I would immediately identify it. I continued with my train of thought, expecting someone to appear within seconds, thereby solving the mystery of the candle incident.

When no one materialized I looked at Mike with eyebrows raised. Mike shrugged it off, and said something to the effect of, "It happens."

Perhaps our candle lighter acknowledged that it was time to leave now that we had arrived?

Michael: The screen door has a hinged latch on the outside that holds it shut. Once it is closed, the wind does not open it. At times, the wind has gotten strong enough on the hill where I live to blow through the screen and force the inner door open. But the screen does not open.

Paul: In any case, I don't recall much wind that early July evening. As I slept less than ten feet away from our phantom candle, I faced the large window in the corner of the cabin, and specifically remember a large moon smiling down. It was a clear night. There was no sign of stormy weather that would produce significant wind to blow the door open.

Mike and I refuse to fill in the blanks, though our lack of a rational explanation does point to potential paranormal activity. We find ourselves between a rational explanation and definitive phenomenon. We often reside in this gray area. We're comfortable there.

While I often had considered the spirit element, I was never directly confronted with the possibility until this experience. I have been a guest at Mike's cabin on many occasions and feel very much at home there. I've had subsequent experiences since what we have come to call "the candle incident" that, while subtle, lead me to strongly consider the possibility there is something or someone there, aside from Mike and me, that generates energy. Whether it be the sound of feet walking across the wood floor while I'm certain that both Mike and I are in bed, a faint and barely audible sound that could be interpreted as whispers, or simply the feeling of being watched, at the risk of sounding sophomoric or cliché, I can refer to the energy as a "presence."

Every so often I try to communicate telepathically to anything or anyone that may be floating around Mike's cabin—a paranormal icebreaker, if you will. When I do so, I'm half joking and 100 percent serious. I was never much for fractions.

It goes something like this: "Dear ghosts and spirits, You guys are welcome to sleep beside me, float around me, and make faces at me behind my back. You are welcome here. I come in peace. Feel free to haunt Mike's house as long as you like. Just please don't reveal yourself to me. I'm just a simple man hunting undiscovered hairy apes, and couldn't possibly handle any other mysteries, so please — no offense — but no face-to-face meetings. I wish you all the best."

Then I'll try to offer something spiritual, "Namaste."

That night after the candle incident, when I lay down to sleep, the possibilities flooded my brain, making sleep difficult. I ran the incident through my mental catalog to find a match, to reconcile the experience by association with something similar I'd already logged in the past. I wasn't uncomfortable. I didn't feel threatened. This was simply new territory for me.

Michael: What Paul's brain was telling him was simply that it was not possible for this candle to be sitting there burning on the woodstove. It was almost inconceivable that we had left it burning, and even in that remote case, it was seemingly impossible that it could still be burning when we got back from our trip. It was almost equally unlikely that anyone had been there to light it within the few hours before we came in. But the only apparent alternative — that some sort of nonphysical entity or force had the ability to set a candle on fire and knew when we were coming back from our trip —

also was impossible for him to believe. His brain was telling him that what he was seeing could not happen. Yet there it was. His reaction to this experience was a softer form of a phenomenon he and I have both observed repeatedly in our experiences with witnesses to paranormal events.

Paul: The psychological impact upon the witness fascinates us almost as much as the subject itself. Our function is not only to prove or disprove the activity, but to ease the witness across the line between what they know and a new and potentially frightening reality. What is most distressing for some is that the introduction of something long dismissed as legend, superstition, or impossibility causes a significant shift in the psyche. Once you introduce the possibility of the previously unreal, you cannot make space for it in your own personal catalog. Everything shifts. The newfound information demands it, and the mind goes about the business of doing so in an almost violent manner.

Michael: In the following pages, we will relate the experiences of many people who have witnessed the impossible, including ourselves and people we've assisted over the years. We will discuss some of our theories about how and why these experiences impact the witnesses at such a deep level. We also will discuss the role of investigators and how we can help these witnesses process their

The Candle Incident

experiences so they can get back to their lives and rediscover peace of mind.

II. The Rabbit Hole Experience

Conflict in the Mind

MICHAEL: At the time we returned from our trip in 2012, Paul held several beliefs that all played together very nicely: we had extinguished all flames before we went to sleep the night before we left; we had been away from the house for four days; a candle, even if left lit, could not burn for four days; no one had been in the house while we were gone. He also believed that it was not possible for a candle to light itself or for some nonmaterial entity or force to light it. The fact that we walked into the house to find a lit candle burning on the woodstove introduced a new piece of knowledge that seemed to be in conflict with at least one of these others. The discomfort he felt that night was not due to fear, but to this conflict.

What Paul was experiencing was a phenomenon known to psychologists as cognitive dissonance. Leon Festinger[2] defined cognitive dissonance as the existence of conflict among the beliefs, knowledge, or opinions a person holds. For simplicity, I will

---

2 Leon Festinger, *A Theory of Cognitive Dissonance* (Stanford, CA: Stanford University Press, 1957).

just use the term "beliefs," but this could really mean anything from what we normally would consider a fact to what we might consider an opinion. All of these are beliefs in which we have different levels of confidence.

In a nutshell, cognitive dissonance theory states that when the things we believe to be true contradict each other, we are psychologically uncomfortable. The degree of discomfort caused by this conflict will depend on many factors, including the number of beliefs that are in conflict and the importance of these beliefs to the person.

It may seem odd that a person could hold multiple beliefs at the same time that conflict with each other, but we probably all suffer from cognitive dissonance to some extent. One way it can arise is when a person has a new experience or discovers new information that is in conflict with beliefs previously held. This is exactly what happens when people experience the paranormal.

Growing up and assimilating to the world includes a continuous process of drawing lines between what is possible and what is impossible, what is real and what is not real. As children, we believe the tooth fairy brings us money if we lose a tooth and that there is a guy named Santa who somehow knows everything we do (but doesn't work for the National Security Agency) as well as a rabbit that brings us candy on Easter.

Conflict in the Mind

Gradually, we learn these things are not true (or at least, that is my current understanding) and we move our inner boundary lines, placing these things outside the realm of the possible. For most people, phenomena such as ghosts, Bigfoots, and UFOs eventually end up on the other side of that line as well. This builds up a structure of beliefs about what is possible and what is not possible.

Paul or I get a call when someone sees or experiences one of those things that are supposed to be on the other side of that line. Maybe a person who doesn't believe in ghosts gets dragged out of bed by something they cannot see, or an experienced outdoorsman who has spent his whole life in the woods turns a corner on a trail and sees an eight-foot humanoid creature staring him in the face. These experiences are frightening in themselves, but in many cases, there's a much deeper impact. Things are not staying on the right side of the lines, or maybe the lines have not been drawn in the right place. New information has been introduced that is in conflict with the beliefs the person holds, putting the person in a state of cognitive dissonance. Like Paul lying on the couch reviewing possible explanations for the candle incident, witnesses begin a process of trying to fit this new information into their belief structure.

According to Festinger's research, when there is a conflict, the discomfort created will inspire the person to take steps to reduce or eliminate the conflict, just as a person who is hungry will take steps to reduce hunger, or a person in pain will take steps to eliminate whatever is causing it. There are several ways this might be done. The most direct way is to change one of the beliefs that are in conflict. If our beliefs were totally flexible, there would be no problem. A momentary conflict would be created, but then the belief structures would adjust: "Huh, I guess Sasquatches do exist after all. What's for dinner?" Generally, though, our beliefs are resistant to change, so a dissonant state can be maintained over time.

Since beliefs built up over a lifetime will be very resistant to change, the first reaction of witnesses likely will be to try rationalizing the experience they just had so that it doesn't need to conflict with their prior beliefs. The person might convince himself he was sleeping and dreamed the incident of being pulled by unseen hands. If the person caught only a glimpse of a strange animal, he might convince himself it was only a bear.

In other cases, the experience may have been so clear that the person is unable to pull this off. He tries to convince himself that what he saw was a bear but he is not convinced. This may leave the person in a dissonant state for an extended period, during which he may take steps to try to reduce the discomfort he is experiencing. He may avoid any information or discussion of Sasquatch and instead seek out other people to tell him it was only a bear, or find experts to testify that many people misidentify bears in the woods. He may adjust his actions so that the conflict is less important in his life. For example, he might decide not to venture into the woods again. The dissonance would still be there, but since he doesn't have to deal with it from day to day, it may not cause much discomfort.

Going back to Paul's response to the candle incident, the simplest way out of his psychological predicament would have been to convince himself the candle was not really lit when we walked in. But as he stood looking at it, this was not an option. It did not correspond to reality. The next simplest possibility would have been to change one of the beliefs that would not require a paranormal explanation. Maybe someone was in my cabin and lit the candle, or maybe we actually had forgotten to blow it out and it burned for four days. Any of these explanations would cause minimal disturbance in the sense that changing them would not need to affect any other beliefs.

The problem here was that they all seemed highly unlikely, so much so that Paul had a hard time changing his original beliefs about them. At the same time, the idea that the candle in one way or another caught fire on its own was also pretty difficult to accept. Paul was in a tough spot. Many witnesses to paranormal phenomena find themselves in a similar predicament, and without the stunning mental agility that Paul possesses.

Case Study: The Phantom Lights of Shark River

Paul: It was a blustery autumn day when I took Koda, my German shepherd, to Shark River Park in Wall Township for a run. Shark River Park is typical of this area of New Jersey—a series of trails through hardwoods and swamp with some gentle slopes offering good resistance for the five-mile run that has become our standard.

Koda and I had gotten a late start that day, and were only midway through our run when darkness fell. Free of the knee pain that has periodically haunted me since my late thirties and inspired by Koda's enthusiasm, I had no plans of stopping anytime soon.

I was on a part of the trail loop shaped like a bowl. To the right of me was a declining slope that eventually leveled off and then inclined up toward another section of trail that was approximately one hundred fifty feet across from me. The trail runs in a horseshoe pattern around the perimeter of the bowl. If I'm running down the trail, I can look across this small valley and see anyone or anything else on the trail directly across from me.

As Koda and I ran, a source of light caught my eye. I looked across from me and saw three lights in a triangular pattern. They looked as if they were directly on the trail. My initial reaction was that it was a jogger wearing reflective tape to avoid getting hit by cars at night.

But as I slowed my pace to satisfy my curiosity, I noticed details. Although it was dark (7–7:30 p.m.), the

Conflict in the Mind

lights revealed enough for me to realize there was no person attached to them or in the immediate area I could see. While the light emitted was not blinding, there was enough provided for me to rule out the possibility of reflective tape on a jogger. As my eyes adjusted, I also realized the lights probably were a bit higher off the ground than the height of a person. They hovered between eight and ten feet.

I slowed to a walk and then stopped. That's when things got interesting. The lights matched my speed. As I slowed down, they slowed down. When I stopped, they stopped. I was now rapt.

When they stopped advancing down the path and remained in one spot, they were still moving in the way boxers gently bounce on their toes—standing in one spot and yet knowing that at any moment they would spring into action.

Considering it was the night before Halloween, my next consideration after jogger was prankster. Yet no one could be seen and no voices could be heard. Of course, that doesn't rule out the possibility. I walked slowly. After quickly glancing ahead of me to avoid tripping over roots, I jogged. I turned to my right and the lights once again were moving down the trail, matching my speed perfectly. I maintained that pace for ten to fifteen seconds, and then, when I got to a straightaway, I took off. Despite my advanced age, I'm in very good shape. At one hundred forty pounds, my body moves without my expending much effort. I could still run a sprint. I'm humble but I can haul ass.

Of course, the lights matched my speed.

The Rabbit Hole Experience

All three were triangular—one on top, with two underneath. Whether they were moving down the trail or remaining idle, they seemed to dance back and forth.

It's difficult to say how long the experience lasted. When one is in the rabbit hole, whether as welcomed guest or unwelcomed intruder, the perception of time shifts. Who has time for the perception of time when one must contend with ghosts, goblins, spaceships, or monsters? When I separate myself from the situation as much as possible, my best guess is that the experience lasted approximately three minutes.

Ultimately, I came to the conclusion that I simply had no reasonable explanation other than this one: the lights were a result of something manmade. Yet I still find it difficult to fathom. At the risk of sounding dramatic, they seemed to be living. Their movement seemed predicated on mine. When I stood still, they stood still as far as their advancement down the path though they kept dancing slightly back and forth while they hovered. That's what made them seem alive. They were like a person who was not moving yet also not completely devoid of animation. It seemed as if the lights were breathing.

Finally, I reached a point where the trail would veer to the right, connecting my location to the location of the phantom lights. Something had to give. After glancing to my right to confirm they were still with me, I stopped running. All three of us—me, Koda, and the phantom lights—were on a crash course.

Until that point, Koda had paid the lights no mind. She was much more interested in trying to recover the trail of a raccoon who'd climbed down a tree to begin the evening hunt, only to turn tail back up. When I stopped running, Koda sat in front of me, turned to me as if to ask the reason for the holdup, and noticed the lights. She stared at them for a second or two, sprung to her feet, and barked. Instantly the lights veered off of the trail and into the woods with great speed, and disappeared.

Since that evening I've run at Shark River Park many times. I made it a point to go back on October 30 the following year, but the lights have yet to honor me with an encore performance.

My personal experience may lack the drama of a knife floating out of a kitchen drawer only to miss my head by inches and stick into the wall next to me or of an otherwise innocent girl's head twisting 360 degrees while she vomits pea soup. But I did experience a moment when I suddenly had no choice but to observe the existence of something I could not classify or deny, potentially leading to a shaking of the foundations of what I previously had perceived to be real.

I called Michael the following evening and relayed my experience. Considering both of our endeavors, his reaction was typical. Other than discussing some of our experiences regarding accounts of phantom lights in books and other literature, there wasn't much we could gather. I continue to run there and have had no additional experiences.

There is, however, one other interesting aspect to the trails of Shark River. Just a few feet off one of the trails in a remote area of the park, there is what seems to be an altar of some sort. Some large rocks placed side by side form a foundation while one large flat rock placed over them acts as a table. On top of the table are smaller rocks stacked on top of one another. A number of smaller stone tables on the ground surround the large one. Perhaps the structure was made by a kid simply exercising some creativity or maybe it's used for some kind of religious ceremony. I like that, in all the years I've been running there, it has yet to be disturbed.

Could there be a connection? I suppose I'm grasping at straws, but sometimes straws are the only things within our reach.

Michael: To summarize our theory so far, when people witness paranormal activity, it puts them into a state of cognitive dissonance by causing a conflict between the experience they've had and the beliefs they've held through their whole lives to that point. They respond by taking measures to reduce the discomfort caused by the conflict. They can ease their minds to some extent by rationalizing the experience and avoiding situations that would expose them to further dissonant ideas.

One interesting aspect of Festinger's theory is that there's a limit to the magnitude of the dissonance that can be maintained. If the psychological discomfort caused by the conflict gets great enough, it will overcome the resistance to change one of the conflicting beliefs or sets of beliefs.

On the one hand, the beliefs held for a whole lifetime, and supported by the beliefs of friends, family, and church, are not going down without a fight. Humans have an amazing capacity for rationalization and denial in order to keep their belief structures intact. A fascinating case study is provided in Festinger's book *When Prophecy Fails*,[3] which describes in detail a group that believed the world was going to end on Dec. 21, 1954. When this prophecy failed to come true, it actually increased the faith of many of the members, especially in the sense of their proselytizing activities to win others over to their faith.

On the other hand, Festinger states a belief is most likely to change if it defies reality. Of course in this context reality means the person's own subjective interpretation of reality, which is all that we ever have. One obvious indication of what a person considers to be real is the ominous phrase we often hear from people who have had these experiences: "I know what I saw!" In these cases, in which the paranormal experience was very powerful and alternative "rational" explanations (those not in conflict with previously held beliefs) no longer correspond to reality, the foundations of the old belief structure may crack.

Beliefs are interconnected. When one falls, dissonance is created with all of the beliefs that were

---

[3] Leon Festinger, Henry Riecken and Stanley Schachter, *When Prophecy Fails: A Social and Psychological Study of a Modern Group That Predicted the Destruction of the World* (New York: Harper Torchbooks, 1956).

related to it. Then they all have to be reconsidered, and so on. The whole belief structure can come tumbling down like a house of cards. In this situation an experience causes a level of cognitive dissonance that cracks the person's prior beliefs about reality. That's the phenomenon we have come to call the Rabbit Hole Experience.

Down the Rabbit Hole

MICHAEL: In *Alice's Adventures in Wonderland* a young girl named Alice follows a rabbit and falls down a hole into a bizarre world where reality doesn't follow the same rules as it does in the world above. Ever since Lewis Carroll's story was published in 1865, the image of the rabbit hole has come to be used as a metaphor for a portal between the world we believe to be real and another world that offers a different reality.

A more modern reference is in *The Matrix*, a film whose premise is that humans live in a computer-created illusion as their bodies are used as batteries by intelligent machines. In a scene alluding to Carroll, the character Morpheus (Laurence Fishburne), who already has seen the reality outside of the Matrix, offers Neo (Keanu Reeves) the choice between a red and a blue pill.

"You take the blue pill, the story ends," he says. "You wake up in your bed and believe whatever you want to believe. You take the red pill, you stay in Wonderland, and I show you how deep the rabbit hole goes."

The Rabbit Hole Experience

The scene can be interpreted as a metaphor for cognitive dissonance. Neo has come to this point because he feels there's something wrong with the world as he experiences it. He is not sure exactly what's awry, but something is, as Morpheus says, "like a splinter in your mind, driving you mad." This is a much more poetic description than Festinger's "psychological discomfort," but the idea is the same. Neo is suffering from cognitive dissonance. He believes the world in which he has lived his whole life is real. Yet there also is a part of him that believes it's not.

Morpheus offers him a choice in how he wants to extract this splinter. He can take the blue pill and go back to his old beliefs, or he can take the red pill, choosing to cast off his old beliefs for a set of new ones he does not yet know. When Neo takes the red pill, he has a rude awakening and discovers the world he has always believed to be real actually was a fantasy in his mind.

From references such as the one in *The Matrix*, Paul and I have come to use the term Rabbit Hole Experience (RHE) to describe an occurrence that forces a person to recognize the world is not what he or she thought it was. When the structure of a person's beliefs has been cracked, there is no going back.

Unlike Neo, witnesses to paranormal phenomena generally don't get to make a conscious choice about which set of beliefs they will hold onto and which they will discard. Probably any paranormal experience causes some degree of dissonance and puts that splinter into the mind. Many people can take the blue pill, though, go back to their daily lives and, to a greater or lesser degree, forget what happened. But those who have experienced an RHE no longer have that option. Many go into a state of shock, which spreads into other aspects of their lives. They can start to lose their grip on what's real and what's not. Others experience something closer to a religious epiphany. They believe they've caught a glimpse of a more beautiful world and feel their lives are richer for the experience.

But not everyone who witnesses something unexplained experiences such a profound impact. Indeed such an effect is relatively rare. Why does a particular situation cause one person to have an RHE while a similar situation does not cause this effect in another person? Why is an RHE positive for some people while causing others to break down in terror and anxiety?

There are many ideas about the structure of the mind, some quite elaborate.[4] A particularly useful

---

[4] Frederic W.H. Myers, *Human Personality and Its Survival of Bodily Death* (New York: Longmans, Green, 1907); Edward F. Kelly, et al., *Irreducible Mind: Toward a Psychology for the 21st Century* (Lanham, MD: Rowman & Littlefield, 2009).

framework for thinking about the RHE is the idea of a mind consisting of two aspects—the objective and subjective minds. I was first introduced to these terms in Thomas Jay Hudson's book, *The Law of Psychic Phenomena*. They correspond to the more commonly heard terms of conscious and subconscious mind, but many researchers of psychic phenomena prefer the objective/subjective formulation because it makes clear the major differences between the two, which is key to understanding how they interact in the context of paranormal phenomena.

The objective (conscious, rational) mind can reason using two different methods known as deduction and induction. Deduction is a form of reasoning that starts from a general premise and follows it logically to draw a conclusion about a particular set of observations. Deduction moves from the cause to its effects. By way of example, if you were to tell me you'd just turned off the stove, I could deduce the burner will still be hot. So I don't touch it.

The reverse process, induction, is a form of reasoning that begins with a particular set of observations and works backward to derive the general premise that must be true in order for the observed phenomena to occur.[5] Induction moves from the

---

[5] Sherlock Holmes, by the way, generally uses induction in solving cases. Throughout the stories, however, his

observed effects to their cause. If I perceive that the stove is hot, I may infer through induction that the stove recently has been on. Both of these methods of reasoning are very useful in helping us survive in the physical world.

According to Hudson, the subjective (subconscious) mind can only reason deductively. So it can take general premises and follow them logically to a particular set of observations and implications. In fact, the subjective mind is remarkably efficient in doing so, far more so than the objective mind. But the subjective mind is not capable of induction, meaning it cannot use experience to work backward and modify or create its own general premises. It can only receive premises from elsewhere. The premises from which the subjective mind starts its work can be provided by the person's own objective mind, known as auto-suggestions, or by the objective minds of others. Once it has a premise, the subjective mind has no choice but to follow that premise to its conclusion.

Hudson argues that the properties of the subjective mind can explain the nature of hypnotism. In the hypnotic state, he claims, the objective mind is taken offline and the person is operating in a "subjective state." (Writing in 1893, he didn't use the term "offline," but I'm betting he would today.) The person therefore accepts whatever suggestions the hypnotist gives. But there is a limit. Hudson

methods are commonly mislabeled as deduction.

claims it's impossible for the hypnotist to force the subject to do anything that would go against his personal convictions. This is due to a conflict between the suggestions of the hypnotist and the auto-suggestions the person has given to himself.

Auto-suggestions do not have to be formal statements. They can be ideas that are built up through experience over time. They encompass an individual's habits of thought as well as the "settled principles and convictions of his whole life," Hudson writes. The more deeply rooted the thoughts, principles, and convictions, the more powerful the auto-suggestions and the more difficult they are to supplant with another suggestion, such as that from a hypnotist. Sound familiar?

So what does all of this have to do with the RHE?

Conceptually, the RHE is similar to what Hudson describes happening when a hypnotized person is given a suggestion that contradicts another: "They are speaking or acting from the standpoint of one suggestion, and to controvert it is to offer a counter suggestion which is equally potent with the first. The result is, and must necessarily be, utter confusion of mind and nervous excitement on the part of the subject."

Further along in his book, he writes: "[I]t is well known to hypnotists that an attempt to contradict or argue with a subject in a hypnotic state invariably distresses him, and persistency in such a course awakens him, often with a nervous shock. A conflict of suggestions invariably causes confusion in the subjective mind, and generally results in restoring the subject to normal consciousness."

What Hudson is describing here is the creation of cognitive dissonance by implanting multiple suggestions that are in conflict. Raising conflicting arguments with a person who is in his or her normal conscious state will not cause the same distress since the person will be able to argue against them in order to avoid conflict. But when a person is in a hypnotic state, this rational process is bypassed so that the suggestions made by the hypnotist become beliefs instantly. If these new beliefs are in conflict with those the person previously held, a conflict is created that causes distress.

As discussed earlier, people will take action to avoid this conflict. In the case of hypnosis, the person can avoid the conflict by waking up and returning to his or her original belief structure.

This is very similar to what we witness with the RHE. Cognitive dissonance is created in the subjective mind by a conflict of suggestions. The difference is that the person is not in a "subjective state" (hypnotized). Therefore, in order for the subjective mind to be affected, the person must have a direct, personal, emotional experience. The subjective mind operates at an emotional level, not a rational, logical one. Psychologists who work with phobia cases know this. A common method used to treat phobias is exposure treatment in which the person is exposed to the fear-inducing stimulus under controlled conditions in order to gradually alleviate the fear. Rationally arguing with the phobia sufferer about why there is no reason to be afraid does not work. The person generally knows there is no rational reason to be afraid. Yet the response does not go away. That's because the premise that this stimulus is something to fear is deep rooted in the subjective mind, and so needs to be dealt with by direct experience.

In the same way, rational arguments about the existence of paranormal activity can never produce the RHE. The person may be entirely convinced in the objective mind that the phenomenon is real, but the subjective mind has not been influenced. As Morpheus says to Neo, "No one can be told what the matrix is. You have to see it for yourself."

A direct personal experience will create the dissonance, but in order for the prior belief structure to crack and a true RHE to occur, the person has to have an experience that leaves the subjective mind no "escape hatch." In this case an escape hatch is another possible explanation for what is being experienced that does not violate any of the prior belief structure. Note here that the explanation only needs to be possible, not necessarily even reasonably likely. Interestingly, in our experience, it does not seem to matter what the objective mind believes about this alternative explanation. It's enough that it exists.

Down the Rabbit Hole

Cognitive dissonance theory even covers this scenario. Since the acceptance of a paranormal element generally will entail changing a lot of beliefs that are very resistant to change, any other explanation that might offer a way out of the dissonance might be an easier target to change. For instance, in Paul's case regarding the candle incident, it is *possible* that we forgot to blow the candle out and it burned for four days. It is *possible* that someone came into my cabin I had only owned for a month, lit a candle, and that we happened to arrive within the few hours that the candle was burning. Paul does not believe any of these things to be true, but they are *possible*. So his mind need not dismantle the rest of his belief structure.

Suppose instead that Paul had actually been standing in front of the candle when he saw it suddenly catch fire on its own. This would have been a very different situation. In that case, none of his prior beliefs would be able to change to accommodate this new information. The explanation that someone snuck into my cabin and lit it would be out, as would any possibility that we had left it lit and it burned all that time. Unless he could come up with some other possibility, there would be no recourse except to admit the paranormal element and all that comes with it.

Case study: The Endless Loop

Michael: One of my favorite running trails is a nice, hilly one on state forest land that spans a little less than half a marathon. It consists of a single loop split down the middle by a dirt road that runs east to west. I probably have run this trail more than a hundred times over the years. I park on the road at the east end of the loop and begin my run from there down the trail on the south side of the road. The trail winds a half loop, crosses the road at the west end, then circles around the north side of the road back to meet my jeep at the other end. Not far from the end of the first half of the loop, there is a section of the trail that crosses through a swampy area over a set of wooden plank bridges. I use this section as a sort of psychological marker. When I get to those bridges, I know that I will hit the road and the halfway point of the run very soon.

One summer day, I started the loop, as I had many times before, down the south side. It was a very hot day, and I was trying to pace my water drinking so I could stay reasonably hydrated but not empty my bottle too soon. When I reached the swampy section and ran over the bridges, I checked my water bottle, noting it was half empty (or half full, depending on your point of view). I decided I would not drink any more until I crossed the road. I continued running. After a while, it occurred to me that it seemed like I should have reached the road already. But perception can get distorted during these runs while my mind wanders, so I did not think too much of it and just kept running.

Down the Rabbit Hole

After a while, when I still had not seen the road, I wondered what was going on. Maybe I was not running as fast as I normally do. Each bend I turned, I thought the road had to be there, but it never was. I was getting thirsty.

Then I rounded a corner and stopped in my tracks. In front of me was the swampy area and the bridges I had already crossed. I stood and stared at them, trying to process what had happened. I turned around and looked down the trail behind me. As far as I was aware, this was not possible. The trail is a simple loop, and there is only one area like this that crosses bridges. There was no way to get back to this spot without circling all the way around the trail, which would have required crossing the road twice, passing my jeep, and covering about twelve miles, which I could not have done since my water bottle was still half full. (Or was it half empty?)

I was disoriented and a little concerned. Part of me worried about whether I would ever get back to my jeep. Maybe they would find me out here days or years later, dehydrated, with my jeep just down the road and everyone would be perplexed about what had happened.

There was nothing I could do except continue running. As I ran, I had a condensed RHE as all of the things I thought I knew about this trail came into question. I had run the trail a hundred times, and I was sure it was a single loop. But maybe it wasn't. Maybe there were side trails that I had never noticed before. Maybe new trails had been added since I ran it last. Was I really sure that there was only one set of bridges? I considered going back the way I came, but I was already six miles into the run from that direction. But was I really sure about that? Did I actually even know where I was at that point?

Once again, I crossed the bridges and kept going down the trail, praying to the running gods that I would not round the corner and find the set of bridges again. As I ran through this section, I noted details that I remembered from running through there before—where the muddy spots were, thorny vines growing across the trail that had to be jumped, the soft spots where the bridges would sink into the mud a bit as I stepped on them. I had definitely come through there before on that day. Hadn't I? It was not just a vague notion that I already crossed the bridges. I remembered the details of how things looked on this particular day. I knew I had been through there before. But was I sure about that?

As I ran, I watched for spur trails, wondering if it were possible I had somehow gotten sidetracked and circled back around without realizing it. I never saw any side trails. Just the simple loop. The trail took me straight to the road, at which point I decided to keep to the safety of the road and run straight to the jeep. I wanted to remove any possibility of getting stuck in the woods forever, reliving Groundhog Day. But I was not even convinced at that point I knew in which direction the jeep was located.

There have been many times when I was grateful to see my jeep again, but maybe never moreso than on that day.

Down the Rabbit Hole

Since then, I have gone back and run this trail many more times. The phenomenon has never repeated. I have never found an explanation for how it happened.

Michael: I still don't have an explanation for what happened that day, and I have to accept that, at least in this lifetime, I never will. The few people to whom I have related the story before writing it here usually ask me what I am claiming happened. I am not claiming anything. I am just relating the experience. I have no idea how to explain it.

But similar stories have been told by many people over the years. UFO witnesses often report gaps of time they cannot explain, such as taking a short drive down a road and finding that it somehow took them hours to make a drive that normally takes a few minutes. Conversely, some people report finding themselves hundreds of miles from where they started, much too far for the amount of time that had passed, with no explanation as to how they got there. In days past, people told similar stories and related the experience to being kidnapped by the fairies. Maybe someday we will have an explanation for these occurrences. But for now, I am very careful with my water supply when I run.

As an interesting footnote to this story, while writing this book, one of my team investigators, Pat, called to tell me a story that one of his coworkers had related to him. The man had been bird hunting with a friend during the day. It was getting near twilight when the two of them were leaving the woods to get back to their car. Suddenly, they both felt a strange sensation and stopped in their tracks. The man says that while they were standing still, they saw the forest "fly by them at 100 mph" as if they were moving through it at blinding speed. The trees flew by in a blur and the stars that had begun to come out were streaks of light. This continued for about ten seconds and then stopped just as suddenly as it had begun. The men found themselves standing in exactly the same spot they'd started. They looked at each other and each asked the other, "Did you see that?" Then they ran out of the woods, got in the truck, drove away and never spoke to each other about the incident again.

The reaction of Pat's coworker is common among those who experience a true RHE. The event lasted only a few seconds. Ten years later, however, he is still troubled by it. He doesn't talk about it, not even with the friend who shared the experience—a typical cognitive dissonance reduction strategy. Talking about it would make it more real. If the friends never speak of it again, it's much easier for them to pretend it didn't happen. Obviously, though, this approach is not working. That splinter is still in his mind. When he and Pat were working together and got talking about Pat's involvement with the paranormal, the man took the opportunity to talk to someone who could convince him he's not crazy. That's a common motivation for many of our clients.

When Pat told me where this had happened — just off the south end of the state forest land where I was running when I had my experience — it certainly made me wonder whether there could be some sort of time disruption in that area. Some areas just seem to have rabbit holes in them. Many theories exist regarding ley lines, earth energies, and other possible explanations for rabbit hole areas, but this is outside the scope of our current discussion. (Note that I am displaying a bit of dissonance here as well by trying to explain the situation as something particular to that spot. So, if I stay out of that particular area, I am "safe" from these things.)

To summarize, the effect we call the RHE seems to take place in the subjective mind. It occurs when someone has a direct, personal, emotional experience that creates conflict in their subjective belief structure and leaves them no psychological escape hatch. In other words, there is no way for them to explain away what happened and keep their belief structure intact.

A key point is that we're talking about the subjective belief structure, which does not necessarily coincide with the rational objective belief structure. The objective mind may believe one thing, while the subjective mind believes something else. It's interesting to think about what we actually mean when we say we "believe" something.

Boundaries of Belief

MICHAEL: Often I am asked whether I believe in ghosts or Sasquatches or UFOs. When we consider this question in the context of the objective and subjective minds, it turns out to be more complex than one might think. It is completely possible to believe something at the objective level while still not accepting it as a premise at the subjective level, or vice versa.

If someone asks me if I believe in ghosts, I will first want to clarify terminology because I don't want to be misunderstood. Frederic Myers defines a ghost as "a manifestation of persistent personal energy," which may or may not indicate any continuing action on the part of a deceased person.[6] I make a distinction between ghosts, spirits, and other nonphysical entities. I prefer the terminology of Hans Holzer,[7] the original so-called ghost hunter. He said a ghost is the residual energy of a person or event that simply plays over and over—

---

[6] Myers, 215.

[7] Hans Holzer, *The Ghost Hunter's Strangest Cases* (New York: Fall River Press, 2006), vii-xi.

what many modern ghost hunters call a "residual haunting" and Myers calls a "veridical after-image." It is tied to a location, does not change its behavior much, and rarely interacts with living people. A spirit, on the other hand, is a conscious entity, generally a deceased human being who no longer possesses a body. In common language, people often do not make a distinction between ghosts and spirits: that's because they mistakenly believe that every "ghost" is a conscious being.

There also is the question of the existence of spiritual entities who were never human beings and never had a physical body. These would be elementals, fairies, and the like. If a nonphysical world exists, then it stands to reason that deceased humans are unlikely to be the only residents of it. When many people refer to ghosts, they may specifically be referring to human spirits or they may be speaking more generally about any nonphysical entity.

Then there is the loaded question of demons. I'm often asked if I believe in them. Ironically, I would say I believe in them in a much more literal way than most of my good Christian friends. I hesitate to use the term demon, however, since for most people it calls to mind the Christian framing of life. I believe there are entities that have no other purpose or goal than to cause suffering to human beings. Some seem to have the goal of dragging humans down to a level below that of animals. But whether or not these are fallen angels, I can't say. They seem to respond to Christian symbols, but whether that is because of their own nature or because these are symbols that people believe in is an open question. I generally speak more in terms of negative or parasitic entities and keep the fallen angel imagery out of the conversation.

Once some common terminology has been established, I can say without reservation that I believe in all these things. I have had many personal experiences that, at both levels of my mind, could not be interpreted any other way.

There also are phenomena that follow logically once you accept the existence of nonphysical beings. An example would be psychokinesis, the movement of objects with the mind. I have seen physical objects move in front of me with no visible cause. If I can believe that a spirit can move objects, and that people exist as spirits after the death of the body, then it seems inconsistent for me to think it is impossible for a person still living, essentially a spirit in a body, to perform the same feat. This is deductive reasoning, and the subjective mind will draw such conclusions on its own. Telepathy, clairvoyance, and other psychic phenomena would fall into this category as well.

I have heard voices speaking directly into my ear when there was no other visible person present. I have received direct responses to questions and requests I have made to invisible entities. And I have recorded these events on audio and video recorders. I would go so far as to say that I "know" these things exist, with the quotation marks representing that it's always possible that I am insane, or have experienced some extremely improbable coincidences, or something else. But at the objective level, I have no rational reason to doubt the existence of such phenomena, and my subjective mind accepts their existence as a premise from which it deduces other conclusions. No skeptic would ever be able to convince me through rational argument that these things do not exist. It would be inconsistent with my personal experience. This is the same sense in which many of our clients say, "I know what I saw."

On the other hand, if someone asks if I "believe" in Sasquatches, I would answer yes. But it would be a very different answer. While I pretty much have taken up permanent residence in the rabbit hole on the spirit front, I have not had such an experience in the Bigfoot field. It's an interesting question to think about what effect a Sasquatch sighting would have on me at this point.

I have seen enough evidence that, at the objective level, I believe these creatures exist. I have heard people in whom I have implicit trust stating they have seen Sasquatches with their own eyes and I have seen evidence of these sightings. There are footprint casts and video that I believe are authentic. At the objective level, the evidence is convincing to me, and I would say I "believe" in the existence of Sasquatches but don't "know" they exist. I have not seen a Sasquatch. So I lack that personal experience necessary to reach the subjective mind and seal the deal.

So, if I were to come face to face, or face to solar plexus, with a Sasquatch on one of our nights in the woods, it would not violate my lines between what I believe to be real and unreal. Additionally, the fact that my lines are already drawn in different places than those of most people (and in pencil) should make them a little more flexible in accommodating shifts. Still, I wonder exactly what effect such an encounter would have on me. Would I experience it differently than someone who is a complete non-believer? Certainly I would have the same immediate fight-or-flight response from a giant man-beast. But once I got home and had half a bottle of Jameson to take the edge off, would I suffer the same long-term effects as others might? It would not conflict with any beliefs I currently hold in the objective mind, as it would with the average person. But would it conflict with any beliefs I hold at the subjective level? I hope I can one day answer this question.

Paul: Most witnesses with whom I come in contact are under the assumption that I've seen, and therefore believe in, Sasquatches. This is not the case.

People are convicted of serious crimes with much less evidence than exists in support of the existence of Sasquatch. But I need more evidence to state a belief. Some may say that my position makes me "less" of an investigator. But I feel that the gray area in which I reside between belief and disbelief is one of the reasons that I investigate: for my own validation. This position grants me objectivity, which I use to guide my conclusions to the best of my ability. Regarding the existence of Sasquatch, I am familiar with, and draw upon, both sides of the argument. This is not a book to prove or disprove any phenomenon. There are plenty of other books that address the issue, pro and con. I think the combination of casts of footprints containing dermal ridges; video such as the 1967 Patterson-Gimlin footage, and the many people I've interviewed all lead me to the conclusion of "strong possibility."

Case Study: Paul's First Encounter

Paul: I was born in 1970, when the shock waves of the Patterson-Gimlin footage were still fresh. I read my first book on the subject—*Bigfoot* by B. Ann Slate and Alan Berry—in 1976. Shows such as *In Search Of ...* were all the rage. Like disco and the Slinky®, Bigfoot was "in." I grew up in Central New Jersey, which, believe it or not, was fairly rural in the 1970s and early 1980s. I lived on a dead-end street, and there were only two other kids close to my age in the neighborhood, so

Boundaries of Belief

I spent a lot of time by myself. Behind our yard were woods with a pond. At the end of my street was a tidal creek that ran into Raritan Bay. Across the creek was a swamp.

While I played organized sports through the township, and had plenty of friends in school, when I was home I roamed the woods, ponds, creeks, and swamps. Catching frogs, fishing, and collecting snakes were all that I cared about. I haven't changed much.

Even at six years old, I was fascinated by the idea of a population of hairy creatures roaming the woods. I suppose it would have frightened a lot of children, but I spent many afternoons in the woods behind my house, all alone, hoping to God that a population of yet-to-be-discovered apes existed.

I was doing fieldwork long before it was fashionable.

And so the twenty-nine years between reading my first book on the subject of cryptozoology and my first interview with a potential witness were spent considering the possibility. Over time I had educated myself regarding the most common points and counterpoints and came to the conclusion that Bigfoots were possible.

So my fall into the rabbit hole was less collision than fender bender. It was cushioned by a combination of books, Leonard Nimoy, youthful enthusiasm and wishful thinking. I got to test my level of belief the first time that I was in Whitehall, New York with a few fellow investigators. Moments after vocalizing in a field surrounded by mountains, we received a return vocal above us from the mountain ridge. That evening I realized that, once any semblance of contact or interaction is achieved, I could no longer dictate the images I had subconsciously forged in the previous thirty years. From that moment on, my perception would be based in part upon factors over which I had no control.

I experienced this feeling a few times during that first expedition when wood knocks were returned and vocalizations were answered. I combined my own experience with those of all the people I'd interviewed over the years, and it was enough. I was in the rabbit hole.

Consider I was not so "high" that I had far to fall. Consider the fall itself broken by years of reading, considering, and hoping. Yet there was still a transition—as subtle as it was—when the idea of something considered by most to be far beyond the realms of what is "real" finally presented itself. In Whitehall I was far removed from my first book on the subject of Sasquatch, but it was there the words jumped off the page and were whooping and knocking their way into my direct experience. I wasn't entirely shocked, as this was the reason that I was roaming a six million-acre wilderness with a group of people I'd never met and with whom I had only Bigfoot in common. Also, I had sought and wanted the experience. Yet I realized then and there I had to give up preconceived ideas I may have dreamt up regarding the subject. As a young boy considering Bigfoot while sipping on chocolate milk, I got to paint the picture. In the field and considering the possibility that I may be among them came an awareness: I don't get to write the script. What if I wanted *Harry and the Hendersons* and got *The Legend of Boggy Creek*?

Boundaries of Belief

Paul: The ten-year-old in me desperately wants to believe in Bigfoot, but my wants cannot be satisfied at the expense of the truth. If one digests the information available, reviews the evidence — no matter how circumstantial it may be — and then draws a conclusion, regardless of what that conclusion may be, I can respect either side of the argument.

If one just denies the possibility while never diving into the crux of the arguments and draws a conclusion without information, that's an entirely different matter. Whatever your stance on the issue, don't allow fear of the rabbit hole to stop you from considering the possibility.

When my dog Murphy and I were heading toward a few hundred acres of woods down the road from my house, I often would cross paths with my neighbor. Bob would be out washing his car and we would exchange waves and commentary on the weather. Hours later, as Big Murph and I made our way home, Bob sometimes was cutting the grass or planting flowers with the missus. From time to time, Bob and I would repeat the same conversation.

"Where do you go?" Bob asked. I described one of my typical hikes: Murph and I slipped off of the road and into the woods, up and down a few hills, across a few swamps, over a few creeks. We'd see deer, hawks, fox, snakes, and more.

"There are fox back there?" Bob asked, his mental wheels turning. You'd have thought I told him there was a small population of Sasquatches back there.

"Sure," I'd tell him. "I've been hiking those woods for ten years. I've seen fox on many occasions."

"I've never seen any," replied old Bob, trying to be as polite as possible while subtly implying I was out of my mind. My reply was always the same.

"They're not going to run across your living room, Bob," I said. So regarding the concept of Sasquatch or cryptozoology in general, regardless of which side of the fence you fall on, don't draw a convenient conclusion from your couch. They're not going to run across your living room.

Michael: In my field, on the other hand, sometimes they run across your living room. I feel no need to try to prove the existence of the paranormal to skeptics (or Skeptics[8] for that matter). Occasionally, I'm confronted by people who will pointedly say to me, "I don't believe in any of that ghost stuff," as if they're presenting a challenge. Apparently, they feel this statement makes it my responsibility to meet them at the EVP[9] Corral at high

_____

[8] The capital "S" here is meant to distinguish the card-carrying members of The Skeptics Society.

[9] Electronic Voice Phenomena (EVP) are recordings of

noon (or maybe midnight would be better) and prove to them the reality of paranormal phenomena. Usually, they are surprised when I respond something like, "Good, then I guess you don't need our help. Call us if you do."

I feel a little differently about my field than Paul does regarding Sasquatches. I do not encourage people to go out and seek the spirit world. Sasquatches are, at least in the psychological sense, a much safer quarry to seek. A person can believe in Bigfoot and, as long as he doesn't spend much time out in the woods alone, that belief does not need to affect his everyday life. Believing in spirits, on the other hand, carries a lot more baggage. It implies that something of us lives on after our physical deaths. Depending on your belief system, this might mean we have to face responsibility for our actions on Earth. It also might mean that while you are here, you are being watched. There may be a spirit watching you right now. Did you just look around? Get this sort of idea into your head, and it is easy to become unhinged. So I see no need to force this belief on anyone.

We are here to help those who no longer have the luxury of not believing. Often they are people who would prefer to be ignorant of the rabbit hole.

voices that are not heard with the naked ear at the time the recordings are made. No one is sure how this happens but it occurs frequently in paranormal investigations. EVP recordings often are used as evidence of a spirit presence.

Many are asking, "Why, oh why, didn't I take the blue pill?" But they have been confronted with evidence they cannot ignore.

While we are discussing our beliefs about Bigfoot and the paranormal, we should make the point that neither Paul nor I believe there is anything supernatural about Sasquatch. There are those in the Bigfoot community who believe that Sasquatches come down in UFOs or that they are interdimensional beings or shapeshifters or something else. The reasoning for this is that it could explain why they are so difficult to find or capture on film. There also are reports in which a series of tracks lead into an open field and then just stop. Advocates of these theories explain this by speculating that Sasquatch was picked up by a UFO or passed into another dimension in the field.

Since I do believe in a nonphysical world, I would not be one to ridicule such theories. It is just that, from the evidence I have seen, I don't see any reason to have to resort to such assumptions when dealing with Sasquatch sightings. There are living primates that are not so different from what we believe Sasquatches to be like. Also, we know that even more similar animals, such as Gigantopithicus, have existed in the past. So it seems the simplest explanation would be a physical flesh and blood animal that has thus far eluded definitive proof. But I've been wrong before. If I should come across evidence that cannot be explained in this way, I will gladly reconsider this position.

Paul: The Sasquatch/UFO connection is a fairly common one, and attractive in part, I think, because it provides a blanket explanation for all that is unknown regarding Bigfoots. It can be used to justify the lack of a body as well as the subject's ability to seemingly disappear. Linking the Sasquatch phenomenon to another somehow may bring a certain satisfaction regarding the lack of explanation. How can we possibly have facts regarding a yet-to-be-discovered creature when it comes from outer space?

I'm not trivializing the connection. I simply don't agree. I can't help but wonder if there is a subconscious compulsion to link the two as a joint classification since neither has been explained to a satisfactory degree.

Bigfoot, the book by B. Ann Slate and Alan Berry, included an encounter with a family who relayed a horrifying account in which their house was under assault from multiple creatures that fit the typical description of a Sasquatch combined with UFO activity. I can't imagine the psychological shift that might take place regarding two separate phenomena revealing themselves at one time. Imagine walking down the road and seeing the Jersey Devil riding a unicorn. This would create a deep rabbit hole indeed.

An open mind is paramount, but I draw a line between what the witness may have seen versus how they perceived their experience and its potential impact on their psyche. If a small population of yet-to-be-discovered primates exist, they are simply that—a yet-to-be-discovered primate. The UFO connection is an intriguing one, however. I can't help but wonder if there is some semblance of relief in wedding one unexplained phenomenon with another as a way of satisfying a need to catalog our experiences.

Perception and Belief

MICHAEL: It's interesting to see where different people draw their lines of belief. Many religious people will tell you they believe in angels and demons and miracles, but they do not believe in ghosts. Surprisingly, I meet a lot of people who have no problem believing in spirits, but think that Bigfoot is a ridiculous notion. It always seemed odd to me that the idea of being surrounded by invisible nonmaterial beings is perfectly reasonable, but the idea of a living animal that simply has not yet been identified is absurd. It's possible the reason is that a flesh and blood animal is something science should be able to prove while spiritual phenomena, since they are not constrained by normal physical laws, conceivably could go undetected by science. Therefore, believing in spirits is "safe" in a psychological sense because there really is no way for science to falsify it.

It's important to consider what we believe and how we believe since our beliefs will shape the way we interpret our experiences. Paranormal events do not occur in a vacuum. Whatever the objective facts of an experience may be, they will be interpreted through the mind of the witness. In other words, how the events are experienced will depend on the witness's background and prior beliefs. The same event experienced by different people will be described in different ways and can have very different effects. What plunges one person down the rabbit hole might seem mundane to another, depending on whether the event is in conflict with any of the objective or subjective beliefs a person holds.

Case Study: The American Monkey

Paul: On the 2005 BFRO expedition to Whitehall, New York, we interviewed a man who worked in a Chinese restaurant.[10] The man, who looked to be between his mid-thirties and forties, recently had arrived from China to work in his relatives' restaurant. An avid fisherman in his native land, he thought he would try his luck in the river that wound through town.

As per the eyewitness account relayed to us through an interpreter, the man was fishing on the river when he encountered what he described as a monkey. Being unfamiliar with the flora and fauna native to the area, he watched the creature, fascinated, yet was not overly frightened. He had no point of reference to alert him to the fact that this creature was by any means out of the

---

[10] Robert E. Bartholomew, 53-54.

ordinary. As the interpreter explained, he had no reason to think a large ape-like creature on the banks of the river was noteworthy. He simply observed the creature and continued to fish.

It wasn't until later that evening when he told his cousin of his encounter with the "American Monkey" and experienced his cousin's reaction that he realized he had witnessed anything out of the ordinary. He had no preconceived idea of real versus unreal, no concept of normalcy to be shattered.

Michael: Paranormal activity does not discriminate. People of all backgrounds experience things they cannot explain. But the cultural background of the witness can greatly influence how an experience is interpreted and whether it causes conflict.

When it comes to spirit activity, religious beliefs also can have a large influence on how a witness responds to his or her experience. An interesting case study involves a member of our team who comes from a somewhat unusual background.

Case Study: Diane's Validation

Michael: When I first joined Scientific Paranormal (SP), there were four of us who conducted all the investigations together and we got to be like family—a seriously twisted family. There was me, the professor; Todd, a paramedic; Catherine, a college student who worked at Victoria's Secret; and Diane, a third-generation Wiccan who was a police officer and part-time model. The Island of Misfit Toys had nothing on us. A fifth member, Chris, occasionally joined us and was a misfit toy in and of himself.

Diane's Wiccan background gave her a different perspective on paranormal activity. Unlike most parents, who tell their kids that there are no such things as ghosts, Diane's mother openly discussed ghosts and spirits with her as a fact of life. When Diane was asked for her fourth-grade yearbook what she wanted to be when she grew up, she said, "A parapsychologist." Unfortunately for her, her teachers didn't think people would know what that was, so they listed "ghostbuster" in the yearbook as her proposed occupation, no doubt making her the most popular girl in school.

Diane's moment of validation, as she calls it, came when she was eight years old. She lived in a duplex at the time, and her step-grandmother lived on the other side of the building. When she passed away, Diane's mother brought in a medium and held a séance. Diane was not allowed to attend the séance, but that night she had an experience in her own room.

She was lying in bed, fully awake (Diane has always had problems sleeping), when she suddenly felt completely paralyzed. She then witnessed a black, shapeless mass floating in her room and her bed started shaking violently. Unable to move, she cried out to her mother, who came running to the room. In order to get her to go back to sleep, her mother told her that the shaking of the bed was caused by the washer and drier even though no laundry was being done in those early hours of the morning. Diane knew the feeling these machines made. Later, her mother admitted that it was not the laundry and that she probably had been visited by a spirit. Diane believes that it was the spirit of her step-grandmother, resulting from the séance.

The experience of being attacked in their own bed would leave most kids terrified. After all, if you can't feel safe in your own bed with the covers pulled over you, you're pretty much out of options. But because of Diane's belief system, she saw the shapeless mass as validation that the things she had been taught were real. She says her mind never ran to the idea that she was not safe or never alone. Since she saw her mother and others going to great lengths to contact spirits, she probably had the idea this was difficult to do. They are not just hanging around all the time waiting to jump us.

Diane went into paranormal research to find answers to her own questions, such as why it seems to be so difficult for spirits to contact us, or why some can pull it off and others seemingly cannot.

She says after that first experience, she felt opened up more to these experiences and became more intuitive or sensitive about them. While I always take claims of sensitivity with a dash of salt, since there is no way for me to verify them, I learned over many cases to take Diane seriously. She always has had a knack for stirring up activity, often because it seems like she is irritating the spirits.

I was present for one significant experience that might have convinced others to drop this line of work. We were investigating one of the most active locations we have ever visited, a place we had investigated many times. On every visit we had captured solid evidence and had personal experiences. At one point on this particular night, several of us were sitting in a circle trying to communicate with the resident spirits. Suddenly, Diane shifted backward and let loose with a long string of profanities. (Diane has a mouth that could make a drill sergeant blush.) She claimed to have seen a white form come at her and felt it pass through her body.

Normally, on investigations, I don't put a lot of weight on personal experiences that are not backed up by evidence. It's not that I don't believe my team members, but if we can't back it up, then it's difficult for me to say what really happened. We have to consider psychology. We are, after all, sitting in the dark in a building that is believed to be haunted. But in this case, another investigator, Jackie, was sitting right next to Diane, and had reacted at exactly the same time, claiming to have seen this thing move past her. Although we did not have a good video shot of the incident, I reviewed the audio of that moment dozens of times to check the timing. I wanted to know whether Diane's reaction influenced Jackie. But the audio confirmed that both called out simultaneously, which leads me to believe that something did, in fact, happen, though I did not see anything. We turned on a flashlight right after the incident and Diane was covered in goose bumps.

This was an intense experience, definitely the kind of thing that could send someone down the rabbit hole without a parachute. But Diane shook it off, aside from owing a small fortune to the swear jar.

She told me an interesting contrasting story about walking around a college campus where she was working with another officer. She is open about her beliefs, so her colleagues are used to her talking about ghosts and such. The officer who was with her did not believe in such things. They were in an area containing artwork by an artist-in-residence when Diane witnessed a black form she describes as being about the size of a computer screen move quickly across a room and disappear into a wall. She did not say anything, but the other officer did. "Did you see that?" he asked. A week later, he quit the job.

Michael: In Diane's case, her prior beliefs told her that spirits did exist. If anything, as a child, she may have had some dissonance created by the fact that she had not experienced anything directly to confirm this. So she experienced as validating an event that would shake the foundations (or at least the bed) of someone else's beliefs. She may have been a little frightened while the episode was occurring, but there were no lasting negative effects. The later episode with the white form was about as dramatic an experience as one can have on an investigation. But she shook it off quickly. Again, it did not create any conflict for her.

Most people who experience the paranormal are not so fortunate. They have been taught and have believed all their lives that these things do not exist. When they have an experience that makes those beliefs impossible to hold onto, they can respond in many different ways depending on the nature of the experience and the framework through which they interpret it. In the next section, we will give some examples of some of these responses to the RHE.

III. Responses to the Unreal

Fear in Two Flavors

PAUL: The most common reactions to paranormal experiences are fear and anxiety on levels at which people have trouble coping with daily life. The initial primal fear doesn't do long-term damage; the secondary fear does. Once there's distance between the witness and whatever provoked fear, any threat, legitimate or perceived, is neutralized. That basic primal fear that has existed since the dawn of humanity—a man narrowly escaping a lion attack—will subside after the man escapes. Despite the danger they pose, lions are a familiar danger. After the narrow escape, a man takes a few deep breaths and is understandably shaken up for a period of time immediately afterward. Then the fear subsides and he goes about his business. But in the case of encountering the unexplained, the psychological impact has only begun.

Case Study: Encounter in the Pine Barrens

Paul: One witness I interviewed described a night in the late seventies when she and her young son had car trouble while driving through the New Jersey Pine Barrens. Despite the stereotypes perpetuated on TV, southern New Jersey is heavily forested. The Pine Barrens encompasses more than a million acres of protected wilderness in seven counties.

Margaret pulled over to the side of an isolated road to inspect her car. She was in the heart of the Barrens. On one side of the road was a few feet of shoulder, followed by a tree line, and then a chain-link barbwire fence. On the other was thick forest. As she surveyed the damage to her car, she sensed footfalls behind her and turned to see a pair of eyes—described as being between seven and eight feet off the ground—looking at her. She noted the broadness of the shoulders of the creature and the seeming absence of a neck, accompanied by the sulphur smell so often described by witnesses of alleged Sasquatch encounters.

Having lived all her life in New Jersey and being married to a lifelong hunter/fisherman, Margaret was familiar with the large animals in the area. She described herself as very comfortable in outdoor settings where she may come in contact with wildlife.

As we go about our business from day to day, we assess and categorize all that we observe. In this case, when she made eye contact with the creature, she instinctively ran the image through her own mental database to identify what or who she was looking at. Her instinct compelled her to identify the animal so she could determine her next course of action, whether it be fighting, fleeing, offering a doggie bone, or simply ignoring its presence altogether. When she ran the image through her database and realized there were no matches, fear kicked in. When she drew the conclusion she was dealing with something unknown, her understandable response was primal fear, which provoked the survival instinct: fight or flight. In the case of an encounter with a seven- to eight-foot yet-to-be-discovered primate, I suggest flight.

Margaret was so terrified that to this day, some forty years later, recounting the story still elicits fear and anxiety. The fear in Margaret's voice was evident even though the immediate threat had subsided decades ago. Yet she still instinctively runs the image of her experience through her own database and continues to come up with nothing. There is no data she can lean on to reconcile her experience, which heightens her anxiety. The first domino fell when she had to call her entire database into question: the line between what's real and unreal had been compromised. The subsequent response was to call into question other concepts that were previously classified as true or untrue, real or unreal.

Remember the boogeyman that struck fear into your heart as a child? He inspired you to sleep with your mom and dad, requiring dad to come into your room and explain there was no boogeyman in your closet or under your bed. As the years went by, and the boogeyman failed to appear, you drew that line in front of him. He (or she; I want to acknowledge the boogeywoman for the sake of gender equality) became classified as unreal. Suddenly, after Margaret's experience in rural New Jersey, that demarcation was erased. Years of classifying images and experiences were compromised in a few seconds.

Suddenly she wondered if that boogeyman had been there all along. Her points of reference were assassinated. All these years later, she can't help but play the incident over in her mind, her subconscious desperate to find a stone previously unturned that will make sense of it all. But to no avail. The votes are in. Try as she might, there is no additional information to enable her to re-establish the line between real and unreal.

Paul: Regarding the initial fear that elicits the fight or flight response, there's an interesting dichotomy between the research that Michael conducts versus the cryptozoological research with which I am involved. Regardless of the fact Margaret encountered something outside the realm of anything she could classify as normal, she was fairly confident she would not encounter the massive bipedal creature in her bathroom. But those who experience spirit activity don't have that luxury.

Michael: Most of our cases do not have such a clear distinction between the initial event and the longer term impact, since the initial event generally takes place at the person's own home and he or she has to deal with it there from the start. Many Bigfoot witnesses will say they will not go back to a particular stretch of woods again, or even into the woods in general. But it is more difficult to say that you will never go into your bathroom or bedroom again. That could get inconvenient (although we have actually seen such cases).

Some people are frightened enough to sell their homes and move, but even so, what they are trying to escape is something that generally doesn't respect geographic boundaries, at least as far as they know. If the cause is residual energy trapped at a location, then moving away generally will be effective. If, however, an active spirit is involved, moving across the globe may make little difference. Although spirits sometimes attach to a physical location, generally a place that was important to them in life, there is really nothing keeping them tied to that place. They also can attach to people and will go wherever the person goes.

Probably the closest analogue to a Bigfoot encounter in the woods that we have in the spirit field is someone who experiences a paranormal event in a reputedly haunted location, but then goes home afterward. In this type of case, there may be the initial shock of experiencing the activity, but the mind can assign it to the fact that this particular place is haunted and therefore different from other places. When the person returns home, which is supposedly not haunted, he or she might feel safe.

Still, it isn't quite the same as the Sasquatch case since, with an eight-foot primate, it's easy to look around the room and determine one is not there.

With spirits, unless a person is sensitive,[11] one can never really be sure. The reaction of a person in this type of situation differs, depending on the nature of the person. Some might go home from the haunted location and be able to treat it almost like they'd been at an amusement park: "Strange things happen at that place, but not at my house." They can avoid the dissonance using this escape hatch for the subjective mind. It could always be a hoax or something else, too. This explains the amusement park or zoo mentality that exists at many famously haunted sites today where people buy tickets to spend the night wandering around, hoping to experience some paranormal activity, and then go home and watch *Real Housewives* and forget the whole thing.

Paul: I am much more frightened of *Real Housewives* than I am of ghosts and monsters.

Michael: My team member, Hayley, reports how she felt after a trip to the St. Augustine Lighthouse in Florida. During a few hours in the lighthouse, she saw what she is fairly convinced was an apparition—certainly an experience that could

---

[11] Sensitive is a term used to describe people who have the ability to sense the presence of spirits. Sensitivity comes in many different forms, from mediums who can see and communicate actively with the spirits to those who just get a feeling that an entity is present.

leave a lasting impression. Yet she did not feel any fear when she went home afterward. She associated the activity with the lighthouse and had no expectation that the spirits there would leave the location.

Not everyone can pull off this little dissonance avoidance trick. A more characteristic reaction for those who have witnessed spirit activity is that they cannot feel comfortable because they never know if they are alone. That's very different from the experience of a Bigfoot witness. Recall that the subjective mind performs logical deduction with extraordinary efficiency. If the person's subjective mind is forced to accept the existence of spirits as a premise, then the conclusion that follows logically is that there is no way to know whether there are spirits around at any moment. Frequently the person will say something such as, "How do I know when I am in the shower that I am not being watched?" (They are always thinking about this in the shower for some reason.)

The fear of never being alone is a big factor for those who experience an infestation or attachment by a negative entity. Perhaps the most terrifying aspect of these experiences is the feeling there is no possibility of escape. The person cannot hide behind closed doors or find a location where they can avoid harm. Negative entities generally will play up this fact for all it's worth by demonstrating to a person he or she is never safe or alone. This is part of a ploy: the person will begin to avoid people they care about so they will not be exposed to the influence of the entity. Such isolation makes the person all the more vulnerable.

But in the vast majority of cases where there is legitimate spirit activity, the spirits are just trying to get attention. They want someone to acknowledge them so they know they still exist. In those cases, it may be true that a person cannot know if he or she is alone, but there's not a reason to fear for safety.

Case study: Coming in from the Cold

Michael: One of the most dramatic fear responses I have witnessed in a client was from a widow in her late sixties who lived alone. Angela called us with reports of activity that sounded serious, but, considering what we encounter, not out of the ordinary. Her husband had passed over recently, and after his death, she reported she'd been sexually attacked by an unseen entity. She had sold the house where the assault occurred and moved to the townhouse where she was living when she called us. The activity had followed her.

She reported hearing footsteps that sounded like boots walking in her hallway, seeing shadows and faces dancing on the walls, and smelling rotting or burning flesh. She felt the presence of spirits around her. Some just seemed sad, she said, but others frightened her. She also felt a sensation on her back that she thought might be a parasitic attachment. Just as in the physical world, there are entities in the spiritual world that exist as parasites. They attach themselves to living people and feed on their energy. If a person is sensitive, she may perceive this in various ways, including as a physical sensation. Angela had been to a few doctors trying to find a physical cause for the sensation but they had not been able to offer a diagnosis.

On the other hand, Angela also reported activity that seemed positive, almost angelic. She told me she'd seen streams of white light come out of her wall and circle on the ceiling in patterns. She described this light show as being very beautiful and very bright though not painful to look at. She felt a sense of peace when it occurred. She also reported occasionally feeling sensations such as caresses on her face and hair, as if someone were comforting her.

At the advice of another paranormal group, she had visited an energy practitioner to help her with the feeling on her back. This person claimed she had pulled fifteen spirits out of Angela. She also told her that the discomfort on her back was an angel wing that was trying to emerge but was stuck. No joke. I could not make that up. Angela and I laughed about this. I asked if she'd come back and help me out if she became an angel, but we thought she might have a hard time getting to me with only one wing.

Despite the ambiguous nature of the activity she was experiencing, Angela was terrified. She was a devout Catholic and tended to interpret and deal with the activity in this framework. Her house was covered with religious artifacts: pictures of Jesus, blessed candles, relics of saints, bottles of holy water. We often find our clients to have these materials, as it is a natural reaction to their experiences under their belief system. To this day, however, I have never seen anything close to Angela's collection. In her basement, where she believed the activity had its source, she had rosaries hanging from the rafters and pipes—one every few square feet. At least we could rule out the presence of demonic entities in the Christian sense. No demon could tolerate living in that house without going premedieval on all the religious artifacts. A person's home is an externalization of the state of their mind. Angela's reflected desperation and terror.

If this were not enough to convince us of the level of her fear, when I spoke with Angela, she revealed to me that for a year or so, she had been sleeping in her car at night. This woman had a very nice home. She did not seem to be hurting for money. Yet, when night fell, she would get fully dressed and leave this home to sleep in her car. At the time we met her, it was November in central New York. She would have to run the heat in the car to keep from freezing. In order to avoid the neighbors seeing her sleeping in her driveway, she drove the car around her residential development, parking in a different place each night. I found it odd, of course, that she thought she could avoid spirits by sitting in her car, especially since changing houses had not brought any peace, but apparently moving night after night made her feel safer.

What was the reason that this activity, which was not all that unusual in our experience, and some of which actually seemed very positive, inspired such fear in this woman? The answer is that she was interpreting it through lenses colored by a violent history of abuse. As a child, she had been sexually abused by her uncle, who forced her not to tell anyone. He had passed away years earlier, and after her husband died, Angela believed her uncle had come back for her.

She also claimed she'd become more sensitive to spiritual entities over the years. It is common that our clients claim to have been sensitive their whole lives. But Angela was unusual. She said that she'd never been sensitive until a few years before her husband's death and that she kept getting more sensitive as time went on. How people adjust when they are naturally becoming more sensitive to these phenomena is a whole other aspect of the rabbit hole. But I don't think I'm qualified to write it since I'm about as insensitive as it's possible to be.

Like many of our clients, Angela had called in other paranormal teams to investigate her home, and as in so many other cases, they had only fueled the fear she already was feeling. She claimed to have had a few very well-known investigators come to her house. Normally, I would be skeptical of such claims, but other things she'd told me that were verifiable seemed to check out. One group told her it had captured a voice through Electronic Voice Phenomenon (EVP) that said that it "would not go easily." Interestingly, they never played the clip for her. She had to take their word for it. I have never understood why a group would come to a person's house, spend time gathering evidence on audio and video recordings, and then never show the evidence to the client, but it is something we hear quite frequently. She also had had a priest come in and bless her home, but as she described it, he sprinkled holy water around from a comfortable place on the couch, and then left. Other priests that she contacted would not help her.

Of course, the most obvious explanation for Angela's plight, especially given her past, was psychological problems. My team members felt this was the case, and looking around the house, one certainly would have difficulty arguing that she was in sound mind. There were, however, also some signs that she was trying to be objective. She told me she had previously watched paranormal shows on TV, but that she had stopped because she did not want her perceptions of her own experiences to be influenced by what she saw on shows. She also was conscious enough of her neighbors' perceptions to drive to different spots to park at night, instead of always sleeping in her driveway.

But the only real way to verify the experiences of a client are not purely psychological is to find some objective evidence to support them. In that sense there appeared to be some validity to some of Angela's experiences. During our investigation, I was leaning in the doorway to the dining room with my back to the hallway where Angela reported hearing the booted footsteps. As I conducted an EVP session with another investigator, I heard what sounded like booted footsteps behind me on the wood floor of the hallway. This took place in November and several of us were wearing boots, so I thought one of our other team members was coming toward us. When I turned around to look, I found that the hallway was empty. I radioed the rest of my team. They were all in the garage and no one had come in. So it seemed at least one of Angela's claims was not purely hallucination.

We also had an odd incident in the living room when we conducted a flashlight session, a technique in which a small Maglite® is used to communicate with spirits. It is frequently seen on TV since you can almost always get the flashlight to flash. We never consider the flashlight responses themselves to be evidence, but we have found over the years that during these sessions, we often pick up EVP or other types of evidence. Maybe it just gets everyone to focus and that somehow enables activity. We had also set up a laser grid on the wall where Angela claimed to see shadows and images. This is a device that looks very similar to a flashlight, but creates a grid of colored laser light. When a spirit manifests, it often takes the form of shadows or figures that are visually subtle and may be hard to see. The uniformity of the laser grid makes it easier to see if something manifests and breaks the beams.

During the session, one of our investigators told any spirit that might be present to make the flashlight brighter on the count of three. Just as she hit three, the laser grid doubled in brightness. Although this was not the flashlight, it certainly would be easy to mistake one for the other. Maybe this was coincidence, but the timing was impeccable.

In evidence review, we found one instance of EVP. As I and another investigator were leaving Angela's master bedroom (which she never slept in), we captured a voice behind us. We could not make out what was being said, but the voice sounded male. All this seemed to suggest there might be some validity to at least some of Angela's claimed experiences.

Was Angela mentally disturbed by her past, or was she experiencing genuine paranormal activity? I am convinced the answer is: both. My own experiences in her home, as well as the evidence we captured, indicated there was something out of the normal occurring. But we did not find evidence of any negative activity. If the laser grid incident was paranormal, it is the type of thing a spirit does when trying to get someone's attention. It's not the behavior of negative entities. Generally, they will avoid revealing themselves to outsiders in order to make the person they're tormenting feel isolated.

Though Angela may have had legitimate paranormal activity occurring in her home, I believe her interpretation of the activity was shaped by her past experience. She saw it as negative and personified it as her abusive uncle. Now that he was not hampered by his meatsuit, she had no means of escape. She was completely at his mercy. In Angela's case, it's not difficult to see why this would be a frightening prospect since she believed that the family member who had sexually abused her was now free to do as he pleased with her at any time. She confided to me that she was terrified of death because she thought her uncle was waiting for her and that when she died, he would take her for good.

In a case like this, investigators need to be conscious of the fact there are multiple issues that need to be addressed and careful not to make any of them worse. Those of us acting as rabbit hole ushers need to have the courage to direct a person to treat all sides of the issue with those who are qualified to do so. This is a tricky business. It's not easy to suggest that clients seek psychological help. They can get defensive, thinking they're being labeled as crazy.

Angela had seen a counselor about her problems and I encouraged her to keep doing so. I explained that we did capture evidence that suggested the presence of spirit activity but that we could not conclude the activity was negative or orchestrated by her uncle. She needed to recognize that her interpretation was being driven by emotions she carried over her past abuse and to deal with that issue regardless of any paranormal presence.

To further complicate matters, Angela did seem to be developing sensitivity, a fact she did not welcome. She repeatedly asked me how to make the spirits leave her alone. I had to tell her that I didn't think there was anything I, or anyone else, could do about that. Since she had some very positive experiences as well, my approach was to instruct her to try to make contact with the positive presences that were around her and trust them to protect her from the darker entities. I told her that she did not need to fear her uncle waiting for her when she died. Since she was a devout Catholic, I used that framework to explain things and told her that deceased family members—her husband, and maybe even angels—were waiting on the other side and that she should have faith they'd protect her from her uncle.

I don't know how Angela ultimately made out. I made myself available at any time for her if something disturbing happened. I heard from her one or two more times, but then contact faded. I don't like to chase clients around too much because it's healthy for them to get back to their lives. If they don't need us any more, then that is a success. I am hoping the fact that I stopped hearing from Angela means she came to terms with things and is not sleeping in her car as I write. Then again, she was not young even at that time. Who knows? Maybe there is an angel with one wing flying around in circles somewhere and looking after me. That would actually explain a lot.

Michael: Angela's case raises another important issue. Investigation of paranormal phenomena, especially when it comes to spirit activity, is complicated by the fact that many witnesses have a history of psychological and emotional trauma. According to the Posttraumatic Stress Disorder Alliance, 70 percent of adults in America have suffered at least one traumatic event, and 20 percent of these suffer from post-traumatic stress disorder (PTSD).[12] For skeptics, the fact that the witnesses have existing psychological issues implies their experiences must be written off as figments of their imagination. Our job as paranormal investigators is to see if there is any objective evidence that something paranormal is involved. The fact that someone has psychological and emotional baggage does not preclude them from having legitimate paranormal concerns. In fact, in our experience, it is quite likely that people

---

[12] "What is PTSD or Posttraumatic Stress Disorder?" *PTSD Alliance,* http://www.ptsdalliance.org/about-ptsd (accessed June 2017)

who do have some sort of psychological disturbance tend to attract parasitic entities that feed on
the energy their condition generates.

Of course, the psychological issues will tend to
shape and often distort the witness's perceptions of
what is actually going on, whether it be paranormal
or not. This was clearly a factor in Angela's case.
Her past experiences of abuse planted autosugges-
tions in her subjective mind that convinced her the
world was a hostile place and those around her
meant her harm. When she began to experience
paranormal phenomena, and also possibly the
emergence of her own sensitivity, she understandably interpreted all these developments in the same
framework.

Obsession

MICHAEL: At the other extreme, some people, after experiencing an RHE, will become obsessed with life in the hole. They may take to spending all of their nights wandering in the woods, spend their rent money on thermal imaging cameras and cover their homes with pictures and reports. True, Paul and I have done all of these things, but one needs to be aware of the line. We still held our day jobs, cleaned ourselves occasionally, and did not alienate (all of) our friends and family.

The obsession response to an RHE has been well represented in films. A good depiction in the UFO context is shown in the classic film *Close Encounters of the Third Kind* after Richard Dreyfuss's character sees a UFO and builds a giant model of Devil's Tower in his living room using dirt and plants from the yard while his wife takes the kids for a one-way ride. Another good cinematic depiction of the obsession response can be seen in the film version of *The Mothman Prophecies*. Richard Gere's character, John Klein (a fictionalized version of John Keel, the author of the book on which the film is loosely based), is manipulated into obsession by entities using the promise that he will be able to communicate with his deceased wife.

Often, these obsessed people form a psychological need for verification, which leads to them hearing a Sasquatch in every twig snap or seeing a spirit in pictures of empty rooms. I often receive pictures that people have taken in their houses that, as far as I can tell, have nothing special in them. Yet the person insists they can see multiple spirits playing Yahtzee. It can be difficult to help these people. When someone wants to see or hear something badly enough, they will, and no one will be able to convince them otherwise. I will just politely tell them I don't see anything in the pictures and leave it at that.

Ultimately, whatever our clients may be experiencing, we would like them to reach the point where they can accept that these phenomena are a part of life and can enrich their lives without taking them over.

Case Study: Ed Opens Pandora's Box

Paul: Ed lived in northwestern New York along the St. Lawrence River in an area with a high concentration of documented alleged Sasquatch activity. He had two interesting encounters. While riding a tractor, he got a quick glimpse of what he believed to be either a Sasquatch or a man in a ghillie suit watching him from a distance.

A year earlier, he'd been hunting from a tree stand in the same area when he watched a coyote, obviously intimidated by something that was shielded from Ed's view, drop a fresh deer kill. He said he saw the coyote with a fawn in its mouth, standing its ground and growling, eyes focused on something or someone. After a few seconds, the coyote submitted, dropping the fawn, turning tail, and running away. Coyotes don't give up fresh kill easily.

Given the area's history, landscape, and geography, combined with the fact we already were working with a witness we had deemed credible whose house was just a few miles to the north, we saw fit to visit the area.

We arrived at Ed's house in St. Lawrence County one late afternoon in early July. We took advantage of the remaining daylight to walk his property, and he showed us where these experiences had occurred. I had interviewed him extensively over the phone, but a personal eyewitness account is much more powerful, as facial expressions and body language help us interpret the mindset of the witness.

After leaving Ed's property we went back to the small hotel where we had stored our gear. I touched base with the other witness. In such a small town I was confident they had to know each other even though neither had knowledge of the other's experience. I explained to each that I was interviewing a local witness who lived a short distance away, and that it may be of benefit to each of them to touch base with the other. Of course, the anonymity of the witness is paramount.

It trumps all other aspects of investigation. Knowing the sense of comfort that comes with the shared experience, I felt there was a good chance each witness would choose to reveal his identity to the other. Common sense dictates that when one has experienced something of this magnitude, speaking with someone else who has had a similar experience brings much needed validation.

Empathy makes for a more comfortable rabbit hole.

They agreed to meet, and I invited Steven to accompany Mike and me to Ed's property when night fell so we could investigate. Before I could complete a formal introduction, each nodded and they shook hands. They knew each other.

After a few awkward seconds of silence, they shared their experiences. We reviewed the details of what both had witnessed as Mike and I periodically interrupted with questions. They compared notes for an hour or so.

Under a full moon we walked the fields behind Ed's house until we arrived at an area where his property backed up to a stone wall that separated his land from a wooded area. We could navigate the fields freely under the moon on our side of the wall, while the cover of trees provided a security blanket for anyone who wished to remain anonymous on the opposite side. My philosophy regarding field expeditions has changed over the years. As rookies, the idea was that we would conceal ourselves in camouflage from head to toe, Army crawl into the wilderness, and with ninja-like skill sneak up on some poor unsuspecting primate, tap her on the shoulder and snap the money shot. Then we'd crawl back out. Game over. I must have spent a fortune in camo clothing and scent concealer used by hunters. If a paintball war ever breaks out, I'm ready. Our approach seemed to make sense. After all, it was the immortal Elmer J. Fudd who would request that we be "vewy quiet" as he was "hunting wabbits."

Over the years we came to the conclusion that if there were undiscovered primates living in the forests of North America, there was a good chance we weren't going to sneak up on them. We considered the probability that, given their intelligence, they probably would associate camouflage clothing with hunting and firearms. We were not going to sneak into their dining rooms while they were having a bite and slap the cuffs on them before they knew what happened. Most interactions between humans and Sasquatches probably would be dictated by Sasquatches who were simply curious. Our approach would be to present ourselves as non-threatening as possible: "We come in peace."

It's quite a relief, actually. The baseball bats, night vision, and recorders are difficult enough to explain to the authorities at 2:30 a.m.

That night in the field we skirted the wall, listening for anything or anyone willing to reveal themselves. It's always good to establish who may be in the area and factor that into the equation. For example, if we hear a pack of coyotes close by, we must take that into consideration when analyzing vocalizations. We sat silently for a while before announcing our presence.

I had wood-knocked twice, with long pauses in between—the Sasquatch equivalent of "Anybody home?"

The Rabbit Hole Experience

We heard some movement toward the opposite end of Ed's property. We'd settled into a corner where his field met the woods near the south end of the stone wall. The noise, which was subtle and faint and yet deliberate, seemed to be coming from the north end.

Mike, Ed, and Steven stayed behind while I walked the length of the wall to locate the source of the noises. I crept about fifty feet when I thought I heard something that aroused my curiosity. I was in a clear field, walking north on the west side of the stone wall, by the light of the moon. I could've read a book. On the other side of the wall, approximately twenty feet away, you couldn't see your hand in front of your face.

When I stopped to analyze the noise, I heard what sounded like a single footstep. I paused.

After a few minutes, I began walking again, as slowly as I could. By my third footstep, I heard the sound again. I continued for another twenty feet, quickening my pace. The frequency of the sound increased to match my speed. I stopped abruptly. Immediately, I heard what sounded like two footsteps come to a halt.

I was not mistaken. On the opposite side of the wall, under the cover of darkness, someone was mirroring me as I walked. When I walked, they walked. When I stopped, they stopped. When I quickened my pace, they matched my speed.

So it went as I walked the length of the stone wall. When I considered the short distance between me and the wall, and tried to gauge the distance of the source, I calculated whoever or whatever it was could not have been more than forty feet from me. If it weren't for the dense woods on the opposite side of the wall, I would have been able to see them clearly by the light of the moon.

I had walked the length of the wall and was making my way back toward the south end of the field where Mike, Ed, and Steven were. Sure enough, my escort was still with me.

I walked diagonally, continuing parallel to the stone wall but inching closer to it. I stopped. It stopped. There was only one thing to do.

I let out a low, quick whistle, almost under my breath. Much to my surprise, within a few seconds, a very human whistle responded, matching mine in both pitch and duration. Damn near perfect, if I do say so myself.

I had a few apples with me. If you show up at someone's house unannounced, the least you can do is bring something. I slowly took an apple, and with an underhand toss, as if I were pitching a baseball to a little kid, I offered it to my new friend. Then I sat on the ground and waited for what seemed like a few months. Nothing.

Of course, thermal imaging would've come in handy, but I'd left it with Mike. You want to know frustration? Go out monster hunting with only one set of night vision, split up, go one way while your ghost hunting amigo goes the other way, and then experience potential Sasquatch activity while he has the night vision. I've been there. Hell, I guess we all have.

I got up and continued walking parallel to the wall toward the guys. My escort did not follow. I stopped walking, waited a while, and began again. My friend remained behind. The first thing I did upon coming within sight of the guys was to account for all three of them. As far as potential whistlers who responded, I could scratch all three of them from the list.

At one point, the four of us traveled north along the stone wall to an opening in the dense brush. Then we split ways. Now on the opposite side of the wall, in the dense woods, Ed and I worked along the stone wall going south, while Michael and Steven went deeper into the woods.

It was slow going. Ed and I traveled ten feet and then stopped to see if I could once again pick up my escort. We did that twice. We walked along at a very slow pace and then stopped for a few minutes to listen. Nothing. The third time we stopped, there was a dull thump—the unmistakable sound of something hitting the ground. Based on the lack of rolling after the initial sound, I considered the possibility something was dropped from above rather than thrown. *It wasn't a rock*, I ventured a guess to myself.

We waited a few minutes, listening. "If you can, make a mental note of where we are right now, as accurate as you possibly can," I whispered to Ed. "We need to find this exact spot tomorrow as precisely as possible. It's extremely important."

We continued south parallel to the stone wall, and then turned to the west as we heard Steven and Michael. Not much excites Mike, but Steven's eyes were as big as dinner plates.

Apparently they had had an escort of their own.

Obsession

Michael: Steven and I were hanging back while Paul advanced into an area from which he had heard sounds earlier. We were trying to be as still and quiet as possible. We were standing in the moonlight but right next to a dense woodline. I had the thermal camera focused on Paul and Ed to watch for any signs that they might flush something else out of the area as they advanced. I heard some faint noise in the woodline next to us. When you're in these areas, though, there are sounds everywhere. I took note of it but was not too concerned.

Then, no more than twenty-five feet from us, we heard what sounded like heavy footsteps in the brush and the movements of a very large animal. When we listened to the recording later, it sounded really loud and close. There is also one other sound on the recording—Steven saying "Oh, God!" It was striking how close it was to us and how large and heavy it sounded. We heard rustling but we also heard solid, deliberate footsteps. I turned the thermal imager on it, but the big weakness of thermal imaging equipment (at least the kind that monster hunters can afford) is that it reads the heat from the first thing it encounters. If you are looking at a dense cover of brush, you get a very good view of the leaves, even in total darkness, but nothing beyond that. We could not see anything. I considered running into the brush to catch whatever was in there, but we were trying to be stationary and quiet, and as far as we knew, if we stayed still, maybe it would come to us. So the audio is all we ended up with.

When Paul and Ed got back to us, I went into the treeline to investigate but found nothing. We had not heard whatever it was leave, but it was gone. I scanned around for any reasonably large animals such as deer or cows but the area was clear.

Paul: I hate to sing the familiar song, but I've been in the woods all my life. Ed and Steven live in an extremely rural area where interacting with wildlife is a daily routine. Hunting and fishing are in their DNA. No doubt they developed at an early age the ability to identify an animal by the sounds it makes—its own vocalizations or the noises it makes as it moves through the forest. These guys do not scare easily.

The four of us reassembled where we began on the south end of Ed's property by the stone wall. As we mulled over the past few hours, we heard an unmistakable sound: two distinct wood knocks. I estimated them to be a mile away.

My expertise in the field and keen sense of crypto-intuition leads me to interpret them thus: "Thanks for the apple."

Mike left a recorder running on the stone wall, we set up a thermal camera covering some food we left as bait, and we went back to the motel to analyze the audio.

Obsession

We returned the following morning. I asked Ed to lead us back to the area where we'd heard something drop. He was confident he could. Under the morning sun, movement through the woods was easier. There were areas where we had to get on our hands and knees, but at least we had daylight. I gave Ed a lot of credit. At five feet eight inches and one hundred forty pounds, I can maneuver through tight cover pretty well. Ed is not economy sized.

"We were right in this area," Ed surmised as we crawled under some brush and emerged in a small clearing. We stood up. The majority of that part of the ground was pure dirt. There wasn't a lot of growth—just thick roots from surrounding trees. As a result, the apple was easy to spot. Based on the sound I'd heard, I was shocked but not surprised, whatever that means.

I picked up the apple, showed it to a wide-eyed Ed, looked above me to make sure I had a space that was free of branches, and tossed the apple straight above my head—maybe fifteen feet or so. It landed a few feet from me, making a sound that was exactly what we'd heard only a few hours earlier.

Upon reviewing the audio from the recorder that we'd left overnight, we were interested to hear the unmistakable sounds of "something" approaching the recorder. It happened immediately after we left. It sounded as if one of our friends was perhaps smelling the small device. When you come across something you don't recognize and need to catalog, you look at it long and hard. The next logical step is to take a good whiff. Perhaps someone out there was having a Rabbit Hole Experience of their own.

The audio had all the makings of a perverted phone call before the age of caller ID. Whoever it was obviously had their mouth right up to the recorder. The only sound was an approach, followed by heavy, labored breathing. Ed's interpretation was not one of excitement and wonder. He was afraid. He heard a primal suggestion deep within his psyche: *This is my land, my property, my hunting grounds. Could I be prey?*

While he continued to work with us as a witness, he would not venture into the woods, even on his own property, without a firearm. Ever since that first night he joined us in the field, his breathing was heavy and his eyes were wide.

Ed's experience had opened up a Pandora's box within his psyche. Suddenly, the dividing line between the real and the unreal was erased. Ed would like nothing more than to simply draw a new line. But he can't. Once you get a glimpse, you cannot "un-see" what you saw. But that doesn't stop people from trying. He continued to pursue the topic. He wanted answers. In fact, he demanded them. I think his demand was more to allay his fear than satisfy his curiosity. His fear didn't prevent him from seeking answers: he was not in denial.

Obsession

Quite to the contrary, his fear demanded that he pursue the issue to reconcile it, perhaps to a degree that bordered on obsession.

Ed had made a vague reference to the fact his interest in Sasquatches frustrated his wife. He was spending a lot of time on message boards and chat rooms debating the subject with others. It got to a point where he was sending us both audio, video, and still photos for analysis. When reviewed, most did not reveal anything substantial.

Given our direct experience at the location, our work with other witnesses within a few miles of his property, a database with many reports from the general vicinity, and the rich history of the area dating back hundreds of years, we feel there is a strong case for potential Sasquatch activity there.

Like Michael's witness Angela, however, Ed began to interpret other benign experiences through lenses colored by potentially legitimate experiences. He was seeing everything through a Sasquatch-colored prism, to use a phrase I often apply to those involved with cryptozoology whose enthusiasm compromises their judgment.

Over time we lost contact with Ed. Both he and Steven, desperate in their attempts to reconcile their experiences, had discussed them with others in their small town. Their stories spread like wildfire. Once this happens, an area becomes compromised. Hoaxers, curiosity seekers, and court jesters come out of the woodwork, and you can't legitimize any audio. Any answered wood knock or vocalization must be taken with a much larger grain of salt because there's a strong chance that the source is nothing more than a bunch of guys "looking for Bigfoot" a mile away.

The blobsquatch phenomenon begins: everyone has a "picture" of a Sasquatch. "See it? It's right there," they say indignantly, as if you need glasses. Meanwhile, you feel like you're staring up at a cloud while a little kid asks you if you can see the duck-billed platypus riding on the back of the brontosaurus.

"See? The platypus is wearing a hat. You don't see it?" It may be obvious to him, but not to the rest of us.

Soon the area becomes so overrun that any potential cryptids wishing to live in peace have to move downtown. Unfortunately, we had to give up on a very interesting area. But I don't fault Steve and Ed for discussing their experiences with others. They were desperate for validation. If one must fall into the rabbit hole, it's at least nice to have company.

Michael: The obsession response is at first difficult to understand. Ed was frightened by his experiences and in no hurry to repeat them. But this fear was overcome by his need for closure. This odd mix of feelings is consistent with a phenomenon Festinger discusses in relation to cognitive dissonance.

Obsession

Ed's experiences were too much to allow him to write them off and go back to his old beliefs. But they were not definitive enough to close all escape hatches. It is possible there was a guy in a ghillie suit out wandering his property. So, despite his fear, Ed's only chance to reduce the conflict in his mind was to gather enough evidence to convince his subjective mind that his new belief in Sasquatches was correct. Of course, what would happen if he came face-to-face with one is a different question.

Wonder

PAUL: Some witnesses interpret an encounter with what they perceive to be an undiscovered primate as a life-affirming experience. They see it as opening a door they long thought was shut. With each passing decade marred with technological advances that seemingly remove all mystery from our natural world, to a select percentage of the demographic, such an experience gives birth to wondrous possibilities. Years, perhaps decades, after Santa Claus, the Tooth Fairy, and the Easter Bunny had been pushed aside by long hours at the office and mortgage payments, mystery and wonder are thrust back into their psyches. The humdrum line between the unexplained and an overdue inspection on the minivan is erased. Unicorns, fairies, and leprechauns are given new life.

Case Study: Allen and the Open Door

Paul: Allen was a great example of someone who experienced "The Open Door." We met eighteen-year-old Allen in the southeastern region of the Adirondack Mountains. We literally bumped into him while in the field doing a preliminary search for an investigation in 2006. As we walked a dirt road, Allen and three friends were coming down the road in his pickup truck. They stopped to readjust hay bales in the back. When our gazes met, he nodded a greeting. One thing about rural areas, you get to know everyone in your neighborhood well. When out-of-towners are traipsing around, it's easy to spot them.

I returned a nod. That was friendly enough for Allen to wander over while his friends secured their load. I quickly sized him up as best I could. Sometimes younger people are a bit more open-minded and a bit less judgmental, so I decided to take a shot.

"How are ya'? Live around here?"

"Yeah, not too far," he replied. "A few miles. You guys huntin'?" I laughed.

"Yeah," I said. "Kinda. We're members of the Bigfoot Field Researchers Organization and we're investigating reports in the area. Have you ever seen or heard anything unusual around here?" After a long pause and a quick glance toward his friends, who were still occupied with their load, he spoke in a hushed tone.

"You gonna be here for a while?" he asked. "I'll come back." Apparently, Allen had a story to tell.

"Sure, man. I'll be here." Then I raised my voice to a more normal volume for the benefit of his friends. "Thanks a lot, man," I said, as if he had just given me directions. "Appreciate it."

After dropping his friends off, Allen returned and told us his story. Almost every spring since he could remember, he'd catch the adults talking about voices coming from the woods. He'd heard the singsongy gibberish on many occasions and said the voices sounded "almost like little kids making up their own language." The adults' conversations were quick and to the point and always ended when someone noticed one of the children listening. It wasn't the kind of conversation fit for mixed company and it certainly wasn't for sharing with outsiders. Another thing about rural areas, the locals are polite but there's a union among them that's seldom shared with out-of-towners.

Allen also had noticed from a young age that if the subject of the voices was brought up, no one ever ventured a guess regarding what they may be. He had his own ideas.

Six years earlier, Allen was in the deep woods surrounding his property. He was building a tree stand in preparation for the upcoming deer hunting season. He was up on a small incline, elevated some thirty feet in comparison to the surrounding ground level, when he heard the sound of movement through the woods. He described the sound as a "crashing." Thinking deer were moving through the area, he crouched down to conceal himself in order to size up the herd that would be fair game in the coming weeks.

What he saw below him, though, was a two-legged creature "no bigger than me" and roughly sixty feet away. He estimated the subject to be approximately three-and-a-half to four feet tall. It walked parallel to Allen's position on the incline.

Allen described the subject as chestnut in color. It moved from his left to his right on an angle, and then made a hard left, moving directly away from the tree stand and crossing an old logging road. Allen was struck by the fluidity of the stride and the length of the arms in comparison to the size of the creature.

"It seemed to glide," he stated when describing its movement. He noted it moved with deceptive speed. It covered ground quickly and yet seemed to move slowly and effortlessly.

When asked how quickly the creature moved, Allen said it was "fast walking."

"Like when you're trying to get ahead of someone but you don't want them to know that you're trying to get ahead of them," he explained.

I asked Allen what he felt in the first second or two he realized he was witnessing something remarkable—something not acknowledged by the majority of people to be real.

Allen explained he didn't think or feel anything. He was incapable. He was frozen with the shock that comes from witnessing a thing that is believed to be "not of this world."

Allen, then twelve years old, fell into the rabbit hole and he fell hard.

As he stood, watching in awe, his shock gave way to primal fear—the survival instinct that has been all but switched off by the relative comfort and safety enjoyed in the twenty-first century. Allen felt the kind of fear prehistoric man encountered daily when coming into direct contact with an animal that has the capability to do great harm. In Allen's case, this fear combined with another—not knowing what the creature was.

Wonder

As he watched the figure move through the woods, Allen's mind searched its database for identification— step one in assessing any situation. While his mind searched desperately for a match to determine a course of action, his body refused to move. His brain, the body's command center, wanted absolute silence while it looked for a match.

The identification determines the reaction. When the figure, still moving away from him, approached a stone wall that bordered the property, it stepped over the wall with ease and simultaneously turned at the waist, looking directly at him. That's when Allen's mind exhausted its comparative search: it had no data regarding what he was witnessing.

I asked Allen if he felt the creature happened to catch a glimpse of him as it turned to navigate the wall or whether the turn was purposeful. When he answered, Allen used the word "intent." He felt there was no relation between the movement required to step over the stone wall and turning to look at him. He noted that the creature turned its body at the waist, as opposed to turning its head using just its neck—a characteristic of movement often noted by people who describe Sasquatch sightings. He described the creature as "expressionless" and recalled that it did not slow down or compromise its stride in any way as it turned toward him. For Allen, that's when shock turned to fear.

"I felt it move through my body," he said.

He said it was as if something hit him at the moment the creature turned to look at him. My guess is that, upon eye contact, the closest match Allen came across in his database was that of human. Yet what he was witnessing, which exhibited many human characteristics, certainly was not what he defined as human. Perhaps he defines it differently now. Perhaps the act of being forced to "redefine" is the entrance to the rabbit hole. Up to that point there was a very distinct line in Allen's mind between a human and the next available match, which most likely would be an ape or monkey. His brain's comparative analysis drew no definitive conclusion because the subject Allen witnessed was tap dancing smack dab on top of that line of demarcation.

When I asked him what went through his mind, his response was, "Nothing. I didn't think anything. I just ran. I didn't say to myself 'Run!' I just started running."

Incapable of thought, Allen's instincts took over. He ran home in tears, feeling a fear that very few people— let alone twelve-year-olds—experience in this day and age. Visibly shaken, he told his parents what happened. We then discussed his parents' reaction. He described his father as "not handling it well."

"To this day, it's not something that we talk about," Allen said, adding that his father also was reassuring, simply telling Allen that he was safe and that all was OK. After Allen calmed down, his father suggested they not tell anyone about what happened.

Allen wanted to clarify for me that his father was not angry about the subject. He was uncomfortable with it. What I found particularly interesting about his description of his father's reaction is that it seemed as though his father was not surprised. I asked if his father's seeming lack of surprise, combined with his suggestion that they not tell anyone, led Allen to believe his father was familiar with the subject and may have had his own experiences.

Allen had considered the possibility and recalled a memory from when he was very young. Family and friends would visit, and they would have bonfires at night for barbecues. One evening his father and uncle told the family to get inside a few seconds after a series of screams echoed through the mountains. Their source seemed very close to the house. Allen's father and uncle, guns loaded, took off in the direction of the screams. Apparently they found nothing, and that was the end of the incident.

Allen had been hunting since he could walk. I was confident that this was no misinterpretation of another animal, particularly after visiting the area and observing his estimation of the distance between him and the creature that stepped over the wall.

Could he be lying? Sure, but considering his hushed tones in the presence of his friends, he certainly didn't seem to be interested in notoriety. He answered my questions consistently. As an investigator, it helps to repeat questions using different phrasing to gauge consistency in answers: "How tall would you say it was?"

An hour into the interview I may rephrase, "Can you estimate the height?"

Allen impressed me. The hoaxers I've dealt with usually are motivated by one of two things. The first is notoriety. "Are you going to post my report on the Internet?" they'll ask. "You guys should shoot an episode of *Finding Bigfoot* here."

The second reason people like to pull hoaxes is the satisfaction they feel after fooling us. They'll get a report posted on the BFRO website documenting their hoax as a legitimate report so they can show their friends they duped us and gain what I can only guess is some perverse and pathetic satisfaction.

Allen didn't seem interested in either notoriety or perverse satisfaction. In fact, he wanted to remain anonymous. He had shared his experience with his parents, but none of his friends knew. As far as getting a report of his experience posted on the Internet to serve as a sorry excuse for his fifteen minutes of fame, he was not interested.

Paul: Allen's response to his experience that day seemed to be almost as fascinating as the experience itself, particularly when I considered his age at the time of our first interview. I got the sense from the change in his demeanor that it had a deep impact on him. There were a few times during the course of the day when our conversation veered off in another direction. We shared a love of hunting and fishing. We discussed how he had fared the previous deer season. Did he prefer bow or shotgun? Allen would speak at a more rapid pace and slightly higher volume when we made small talk over how many turkeys he'd shot that spring. When I re-introduced the topic of his experience back into the conversation, his eyebrows lowered and his voice got deeper and quieter.

Wonder

We spent most of the day with Allen, and it was hours later when he exclaimed, "Oh, yeah! I got something else to show ya'." He disappeared into the house. In a few minutes he reappeared holding a digital camera and scrolling through a set of pictures. "There it is," he muttered. "Look at this." He passed me the camera. It was a photo of a very large footprint in mud. "I found it last spring after a rain."

Allen's foot was next to the print for a size comparison. The print made Allen's size ten boot look like something that should be hanging off my rear view mirror.

He and I also talked about how these experiences affected him. Interestingly, Allen was not terrorized, as are so many people, including Margaret, who've had similar encounters. Nor was he compelled to make sense of what happened and pursue it further as so many other witnesses understandably do, including Ed from Northwestern New York. Despite his fear, Ed plunged headfirst into his own quest for answers to validate his experience, dedicating a significant amount of time and effort.

Margaret's only option was to suppress the experience. When our conversation began, she read my mind as I quickly became aware of how much the experience still affected her. Despite how grateful I was that she took the time to speak with me, I also couldn't help but wonder why she was interested in reliving something so traumatic. She explained she was hoping for cathartic release. She had suppressed the memory for a long time. Fear thrives under cover of darkness but often dies when exposed to the light of truth.

Suppression is a desperate and often vain attempt to hold onto sanity by avoiding the need to reconcile an experience. Witnesses who suppress keep their memories bound and gagged in the basement of their minds.

On the surface, it can seem that Ed's approach of embarking on a personal crusade for validation is more healthy. Exploring the question can simply be a matter of self-preservation. But the exploration can be taken to extremes. The crusade can become an obsession, as Mike mentioned when he used the *Close Encounters of the Third Kind* analogy. To read up on the subject and gain a better understanding is healthy, provided one doesn't sacrifice job, marriage, or quality of life in the process.

Allen's response was unique in comparison. When I asked him to sum up his experience, he told me he didn't feel a need to prove to the world that these creatures exist. It didn't matter to him. I asked him if he now hesitated to walk his property alone, or if he refused to go too far from the house at night.

"No," he said. "If anything, I'm more aware. I make more of a point to look around as I'm walking, but I think it's just as much out of respect as anything else. I don't want to intrude.

"I don't really care if people believe in them or not because their beliefs don't change what happened to me that day. I saw what I saw. Why do I need to convince people? They're probably just animals with the same needs as we have. They're probably better off without us."

Allen's view was interesting. He wasn't particularly frightened. He wasn't inspired to validate his experience by converting people.

"Are you glad that you had that experience?" I asked. "Was it positive?" He looked off in the distance, mulling over the question before smiling. He nodded.

"Yeah," he said. "It was."

For Allen, the experience opened a very private doorway to other possibilities.

Ten years after our initial interview, I reached out to Allen via social media. I explained the project that Michael and I were working on and asked if he wouldn't mind revisiting his experience. He was then a busy man with a wife and a baby on the way. He agreed, and after an extensive game of phone tag, I interviewed Allen again in 2015. Using the notes I recorded in our initial interview as a point of reference, and taking additional notes as we spoke, I was amazed at how his story was consistent with the one he had relayed a decade earlier.

He shared with me that, up until I had reached out to him again so many years later, he had never shared his experience with his wife. But after the first of our series of phone calls in 2015, he felt the need to tell her. Interestingly, she shared with him her own experience that she had as a teenager while in the car with her mother. I told him I'd be interested in interviewing her at some point. He agreed, but a few subsequent requests afterwards went unanswered. He was a new husband and father with new priorities. It seemed an important chapter in his life but just one chapter nonetheless. After two or three texts requesting an interview with his wife, I let go.

Allen obviously had. He sought no notoriety; in those ten interim years we'd had zero contact with each other. He never called me with requests to appear on TV, emailed me with suggestions regarding a movie, or asked if he could appear on our website. Simply grateful for the experience, Allen had moved on with his life.

Initially he had fallen into the rabbit hole, but he is now comfortable there. After reconciling on his own, Allen walked through the open door.

Denial

MICHAEL: In previous sections we described the common reactions of fear and obsession. At the other extreme are people who go into denial. They'll tell you the experience never happened, and that's that. Generally, they will not talk about it. They may even ridicule others who report having similar experiences as a defense mechanism. This response is common for UFO witnesses, as observed by UFO researcher Jacques Vallée:

> *Witnesses of UFO's are generally characterized by their silence. As if they had experienced a very bad or revolting dream, they talk only reluctantly about it, both because some of them remain nonbelievers and are shocked by their seeing something which does not agree with their reason, and because they suddenly find themselves on the other side of the fence.*[13]

---

[13] Jacques Vallée, *Anatomy of a Phenomenon: Unidentified Objects in Space – A Scientific Appraisal* (Chicago: Henry Regnery, 1965), 119.

The denial response is a dissonance control mechanism. It's like the old joke where the guy says to his doctor, "My arm hurts when I move it like this" and the doctor responds, "Then don't move it like that." That's the gist of the strategy: avoid any talk about the paranormal, or any exposure to evidence, and don't think about it.

Paul and I have found that the denial response is more common in the Bigfoot field than in spirit work. The nature of Sasquatch activity, as with most UFO cases, is that there is a separation between the context of the experience and the witness's everyday life. Once the person is safe at home, it is easier to deny the event ever occurred. When activity is taking place in someone's house, it is more difficult to deny. If the activity is fairly mild and not directly affecting a family's daily life, they may just ignore it. I have seen many cases in which children are reporting activity. When the parents actually have an experience, they deny it and tell the children not to talk about it.

For people who've truly had an RHE, denial seems unlikely to work in the long term. The subjective mind knows what it saw and the belief structure has been cracked. The person is living in a dissonant state that probably will manifest in other issues later. It would make for an interesting study to follow such people, though one seems unlikely since the fact these people are denying the experience means they probably will not report it.

Case Study: Four Apartments, Five Rabbit Holes

Michael: One case I investigated presented a very interesting variety of reactions to the rabbit hole all in one place. The location was a building that had been divided into four apartments, one on each side of the building on the ground level, and one directly above each of these on the second floor. The building was split vertically, so that you had to go outside in order to access the entryway of the apartments on the other side. The two ground-floor apartments had access to a common basement. Each of the top-floor apartments had an attic space above it, but the attics were not connected.

We got the original call from the sister of a woman who lived in the ground-floor apartment on the south side of the building with her husband and two children, one boy and one girl. At the time of our initial investigation, the boy was about three years old and his sister between one and two. The family had contacted us out of concern for their children. The boy kept telling them a little girl (not his sister, who was too young for this) came to his room at night and would not let him sleep. He said the girl's name was Katie. She would jump up and down on his bed and try to get him to play.

But Katie's activities were more than just annoying. The boy began to act up and whenever he got into trouble, he told his parents that Katie had told him to do things. In one incident, he tried to hold his sister's head under the water when they were in the bathtub

119

and then claimed he did so on Katie's instruction. Apparently, when he did not follow Katie's instructions, she would get upset. One night, he came running out of his room screaming that Katie had scratched his stomach, and his parents found a fresh scratch mark there. The family called us in to see if there was any truth to his story and to figure out if their children were in any danger.

The client's sister, who originally had called us but did not live in the building, liked to watch ghost shows and had tried to investigate things one night. She and a group of friends had gone into the basement and tried to communicate with any spirit that might be there. They reported seeing a soda can launch off a sink and having one member of their group attacked by an unseen force and having her shirt torn. While we listen to these stories to give us background information, we can never take them at face value because stories tend to get distorted in memory and retelling.

It didn't take long to realize that the family's little boy was not making up stories. Despite the fact all of the children had been taken elsewhere for the night, I started hearing a child's voice before we'd even finished setting up our equipment. Usually, when my team members are seeing and hearing phenomena on investigations, things seem perfectly quiet to me. But this voice was right out loud. I had my ear to the vents and walls as I tried to figure out where it was coming from, but I could not locate a source.

Once we had set up, Catherine and I conducted an Electronic Voice Phenomenon (EVP) session in the living room. EVP is a phenomenon in which a voice that is not heard in real time with the naked ear is captured on recording devices. No one really knows how this occurs. Many researchers, myself included, believe that the reason the voice is not heard at the time is that it is not actually a sound wave. Instead, a spirit is somehow able to imprint an electromagnetic signal onto a device as information, bypassing sound and the microphone. Paranormal investigators often will try to communicate with spirits by sitting in a room and asking questions while leaving time between the questions in hopes that spirits might imprint answers on the recorders that may be heard when the recordings are reviewed later.

Voices that are heard through the naked ear at the time they are recorded are not, strictly speaking, classified as EVP, and are in my experience far more rare. But that was the case during this investigation. Several times after asking a question, we heard a child's voice, but it sounded distant, and Catherine kept going to the front door to see if there were any children outside. We were able to capture the voice on recorders as well.

On review of our audio recorders later, we also captured some true EVP that we did not hear at the time. Most disturbing was that we picked up a child's voice saying "Daddy!" while Catherine and I were in the basement alone. We did not hear anything at the time. On a subsequent investigation, we picked up the same voice saying "Daddy!" Only that time it was in the apartment on the second floor. This rules out that it could have been some sort of mechanical noise that just sounded like a voice. Since I was the only male in the room in both cases, it seems that Katie has adopted me as her foster father. She at least does not eat much.

Our client and her family were understandably frightened by the activity. Our validation of it through our own experiences and recordings verified to them that their son was, in fact, being visited by a spirit. Given some of the things this spirit had been telling him to do, their fear was certainly understandable. They wanted to move out but finances made that difficult. Later, when the husband died of chronic illness during the period when we were still working this case, the rest of the family did move.

In the apartment above our client's, there lived a single mother with a young boy. She had an attic directly above her apartment, and the only access to it was through her living room. We interviewed her, and she reported occasionally hearing what sounded like a child's voice. She also said that at night, she would hear things moving in the attic—loud sounds as if furniture was being dragged around. But whenever she checked the attic, nothing seemed to be moved. We spent the night in this apartment on one occasion and heard the attic noises, so this woman was experiencing legitimate paranormal activity.

The woman's son, who was roughly the same age as our client's son, also reported being visited by a little girl. Supposedly, she and her son were not aware of the claims of the client downstairs though that's difficult to verify with people living in the same building. While the second-floor woman experienced some of the activity, she was not overly concerned about it. Being a single mother took up all her thought and energy: she just did not have time to worry about such things. Due to her personal situation, she and her son did not spend all weekends at the apartment, so it was easier for her to ignore the activity. She did not seem to be denying the activity out of a dissonance reaction.

The north side of the building did not seem to experience much of the activity that occurred on the other side. The top floor was the home of a woman I will call Melissa who had experienced some of the activity, both while visiting the residents of the south side downstairs and to a lesser extent in her own apartment. Melissa felt sorry for the little spirit girl and wished the girl would come over to her place more. She had no fear at all of the activity and desired to experience more of it, but for whatever reason, Katie seemed to keep mostly to the other side of the building. It may be she was attracted by the presence of the family's children. Melissa's niece would occasionally come to stay with her, and her niece told her that when she stayed there, a little girl would come to her room and sing to her at night. But most of the time, Melissa's place was quiet.

In the fourth apartment, on the first floor of the north side, lived a couple who we rarely saw in our time at the location. They knew we were there and what we were up to, but they wanted nothing to do with it. They declined requests to be interviewed by my team about anything they might have experienced. When we investigated the building, which we did on multiple occasions, all of the other residents cleared out for us so that we could have the run of the building. This couple did not. They stayed in their apartment and were quiet throughout the night. I don't know if they ever experienced activity in their apartment. They were not willing to talk to us about it.

Of course, this raises the question of whether this couple was hoaxing the activity. But this was an older couple that just kept to themselves. They were certainly not running around this building at night making noises in the attic and then sneaking into another area to project voices. In any case, there would be no way to get away with it when we had cameras covering the whole building. They simply wanted nothing to do with us.

This is a fairly common reaction to the rabbit hole. Some people are so protective of the lines they have drawn that they do not want to even talk to anyone who might smudge them. Maybe these people were religious and did not want to cross forbidden lines. Maybe they were just plain afraid. Or maybe they just thought we were crazy (not a completely unreasonable assumption).

These people lived in one of the most legitimately haunted buildings I have ever investigated, and it seemed like their way of keeping from falling into the rabbit hole was to keep the doors locked and not talk to anyone about any of it. Some people just don't want to go there. That is OK. Start moving those lines and things can get out of control pretty quickly. It's not for everybody.

So four families, four apartments. What's with the fifth rabbit hole? That's a reference to the experience of Hayley, a member of my team. As with many of our members, Hayley had never had a real paranormal experience prior to joining SP. She was a fan of *Ghost Hunters* and it raised unanswered questions for her that she wanted to investigate. So she joined us. Many investigators can go for years without ever having a significant paranormal experience. Hayley was fortunate enough to spend her second investigation sleeping overnight in this building.

As she describes it, she did not have any significant experiences during the active investigation period. It was when we tried to go to sleep that the rabbit hole opened for her.

We had investigated into the wee hours of the morning and it was 4 a.m. before we settled down to sleep in the upstairs apartment where sounds were heard in the attic above. Catherine and Hayley slept in the living room, which contained the only door leading to the attic. I was set up in the dining room, which was connected to the living room by an archway.

About a half hour after we settled down, I heard Katie's voice. There were absolutely no (living) children in the building that night. I listened to the voice for about twenty minutes. It sounded faint, but I could not pinpoint the direction from which it came. Hayley heard it, too. It sounded to her like it was coming from the room where I was sleeping. Catherine was asleep at this point. Catherine could sleep at the gates of Hell.

Hayley describes the voice as faint, but not distant, and sounding like a child. Since I was the only one in the dining room, and there was no one else on that side of the building other than the three of us, she had no explanation for what she was hearing. After listening for a while, she wanted someone else to validate what she was hearing to make sure she wasn't crazy.

"Is anyone else hearing that?" she asked.

"Yes," I answered.

"It sounds like a little girl," she added.

"Yes," I said. After 4 a.m. my conversational skills are not at their peak.

Shortly afterward, we heard sounds of things being dragged around in the attic above. These were loud sounds that could not be mistaken for animals in the attic or anything else we could think of. Hayley described them later as noises that would be made by someone moving a couch or something of similar size. The only access to the attic was through a door in the room in which Catherine and Hayley were sleeping. I decided to go up there and set up a camera to see if we could catch anything actually moving. As soon as I went up the stairs to the attic, all the noise stopped.

I settled back into my sleeping bag, and about ten minutes later, we heard Katie's voice again. Katie came right up to my head and was speaking directly into my ear. Her voice came through as if through earplugs plugged into an iPod lying next to my head. It sounded faint, but I could tell it was not far away. I could not make out what she was saying, and I did not utter a word to any of my teammates. Understandably, Hayley already was a little freaked out. To my surprise, when I went over the recordings, I heard Katie's voice on a recorder that was ten feet away from where I was sleeping. For the most part, it is impossible to make out what she is saying. But there is one point where she seems to ask, "Can you hear me?" I still get emotional when I listen to it, thinking of this little girl standing right next to me trying desperately to communicate with me.

Hayley also thought she saw a shadow standing over Catherine by her feet. Catherine, who had descended into the rabbit hole long before, had been sleeping soundly through much of this. Hayley woke Catherine to tell her that she saw someone standing over her. Catherine responded that her feet felt very cold but she did not see anything.

Interestingly, this visual experience did not have the same impact on Hayley as the sounds she was hearing. As she recalls it, even at the time, she was not sure what she had seen. She says it was dark and she did not have her glasses on, so she thought she might be mistaken. Such experiences are common, but they do not have the rabbit hole effect since they can so easily be explained away without any lines being crossed.

Hayley says that after we left the next morning, it took her a few days to process what she had experienced. It did not impact her right away. But after a few days, she began to think back on what she'd heard, and wondered, *Did I really hear a ghost?* The fact Catherine and I also had been there and experienced the same thing validated it for her. But she says that had she been alone, she would have been able to convince herself she'd been mistaken in some way. This is interesting. Despite the fact that, in my opinion, Hayley heard the voice of a spirit that night, and despite the fact that, at the objective level, she believes in such things, her prior belief structure was left intact. The fact that validation from others is necessary to support her belief that she heard a spirit indicates she was not convinced at the subjective level.

Contrast that response with the witnesses who say, "I know what I saw." They believe in what they saw despite the views of others.

Michael: As time went by, Hayley questioned her memory more and more. She wondered if she'd heard something else. Maybe she'd been mistaken. I asked if the recordings impacted how she felt. She said hearing them reminded her of that night and validated that she hadn't imagined it. But there was enough distance between her experiences and the recordings that her mind could keep the two separate.

Hayley has worked many more investigations over the years. Surprisingly, she believes she is actually more skeptical now than she was then because she has seen, over and over again, how people can misinterpret what they experience as something paranormal when it may have a perfectly mundane explanation. When team members get more skeptical with each investigation, I take this as a sign I am running the team properly.

Still, what Hayley experienced was legitimate. I have spent time in that building on several other occasions and heard the same voice each time. It corresponds with the claims that the clients presented to us and we have captured the experiences on recorders. Hayley heard the voice of a spirit that

Denial

night but it did not trigger a Rabbit Hole Experience for her. Though her objective mind is convinced she heard a ghost, her subjective mind was left with an escape hatch. The premise that ghosts are not real is, at some level, intact, and therefore, her subjective mind deduces, it must have been something else she heard, despite her objective belief.

IV. Investigating the Rabbit Hole

Techniques and Timing

MICHAEL: When we are called by a witness to conduct an investigation, we have two complementary goals in mind. The first is accumulating information that will give us a better idea of what's going on at the location. This may mean evidence of a paranormal nature, or it may mean information that can point to more ordinary causes for the reported activity. Either way, we want to get to the bottom of clients' experiences.

A second, and at least equally important, goal is to help clients psychologically. We want to reduce the dissonance they are experiencing, and, if they have inadvertently swallowed the red pill, ease their fall down the rabbit hole. This is true whether or not we ultimately may believe there is anything paranormal taking place at the location. In some cases, there is legitimate paranormal activity occurring. In others, we may suspect that the causes may be more mundane.

In either case, though, the witnesses believe they have experienced something out of the ordinary, and we have to approach it from that standpoint regardless of the true cause.

For both of these goals, it is important that we re-create, as closely as possible, the conditions under which the client has experienced activity. This answers one of the questions paranormal investigators are frequently asked: "Why do you have to do your investigations at night in the dark? Don't ghosts come out in the daytime?" Many people think we do our work at night to create a spooky atmosphere. Prominent Skeptic Ben Radford calls this approach the "stakeout" method of investigation and states that it is "a sure sign of pseudoscience and amateur investigation."[14]

But there are good practical reasons why we do most of our work at night. There are theories about the "witching hours" or sidereal time periods in which activity is more frequent. They may be true. But it's also true that at night, things are quiet, there are fewer distractions, and people notice things more. There's also the primal human fear of the dark. Regardless of the reasons, the majority of experiences of a paranormal nature are reported to occur at night and we want to re-create the circumstances under which clients experienced the activity. If they are seeing shadows or hearing voices at night, there is no way for us to draw any conclu-

---

[14] Benjamin Radford, *Scientific Paranormal Investigation: How to Solve Unexplained Mysteries* (Corrales, NM: Rhombus Publishing, 2010).

sions about what's happening by visiting their home at lunchtime.

Sometimes we do conduct investigations in the daylight, though. In one case, we were called in to investigate a café owned by two women. They were the ones who opened in the morning, and they were the ones who locked up in the afternoon, usually around 2 p.m. Before they left, they would check the place, making sure everything was off and put away. But on multiple occasions, they came back in the morning to find a burner to the gas stovetop on full blast and the whole building heated up to nearly one hundred degrees. There were no signs anyone had broken into the café. Understandably, the owners were concerned not only about the gas bill but about the danger of fire taking away their livelihood.

In this case, I had no compelling reason to assume the stove was turning on in the wee hours of morning. For all we knew, if the cause was paranormal, the burner could be turning on right after they walked out the door in the afternoon. My approach was to arrive as they closed up and run cameras and recorders from the moment they left until the time they returned in the morning. We did an active investigation of the place during the night since that was a time when the streets were quiet and it was easier to do EVP work. But our equipment ran from afternoon to morning—some eighteen hours in total.

Interestingly, there's a history of mysterious fires in the small town in which the café is located, which makes this phenomenon all the more curious. This case has not been resolved. The last time we heard from the clients, they were setting up their own digital video recorder (DVR) in the café to record constantly and see if they could catch the burner turning on.

On a different case elsewhere, a family reported that around 3 o'clock on many afternoons, a shadowy figure walked past the window of their living room. Originally, they mistook it for the mailman, but then they started getting up to look out the window when it passed, and there was never anyone around. Naturally, for this case, I was there with cameras set up at the designated time, though I never did see the apparition described.

But in the vast majority of cases, we investigate the location in the dark and try to re-create the conditions of the experiences, even to the extent of having the same people present. It could be that some people are attracting the activity.

Paul: In regard to investigating reports of Sasquatch activity, the complementary goals are the same.

First, after drawing the conclusion that the person in question believes whatever they saw to be real, we assess the situation, first via phone interview. At the outset we want to rule out logical explanations, such as indigenous wildlife. Then there's the matter of misinterpretation to consider. Any evidence submitted is examined. Unfortunately, though, most reported sightings are made by people who are ill prepared to run into a yet-to-be-discovered primate. Cell phone cameras are ineffective when operated by the shaky hand of someone convinced they are seeing something of such magnitude, and undiscovered primates are notorious for being uncooperative when it comes to posing for pictures. Evidence submitted is often compelling but also, in my experience to date, never definitive.

Our second goal is to provide dissonance reduction and a soft landing into the rabbit hole. What separates the investigation of Sasquatch reports from accounts of spirit activity is that the latter has the potential to continue indefinitely. There may be a reason that a spirit/entity has chosen a particular area and is unwilling to leave. The client may be faced with a chronic inhabitant hell-bent on staying put.

In regard to the Bigfoots, those who have testified to having face-to-face encounters only meet a Sasquatch once. Allen is a great example. Despite living in a sparsely populated area between two tracts of wilderness encompassing millions of acres, and describing many situations in which he experienced the feeling of being watched, he had only one direct encounter. No one's going to call an emergency Bigfoot hotline and send me screeching down the road to pick up the hot trail and catch our friend eating out of the garbage can. While there are many reports of Bigfoots returning to the scene of a crime, they tend to get while the getting is good.

I like to conduct the initial interview of a witness and survey the property in the daytime to assess the general landscape and identify potential tracks. But when it comes to making contact, we try at night. While scores of sightings have been reported in the daytime, the general consensus is that the potential for experiencing Sasquatch activity is greater at night. Whether that's because they're nocturnal, emboldened in the shadows, or a combination of both is open to discussion.

The Role of Evidence

MICHAEL: Often skeptics ask paranormal researchers to produce proof of paranormal activity. The assumption behind this request is that there could exist some form of evidence that would be completely objective and therefore be convincing to anyone to whom it was shown. Essentially, they're looking for a mobile, reproducible RHE production device. But this is not the nature of the beast.

Evidence always exists within a context. Something that may be convincing to me because I was there at the time, and know all the conditions under which it was captured, might not be convincing at all to anyone who was not there. I know I feel this way whenever clients send us EVP or photos they have taken in their home. We look at them. We listen. But without knowing all the conditions under which they were produced, we have to take them with some seasoning.

I suppose that in the Bigfoot world, a body might be this kind of proof. Even here I am not confident, though. The human mind has an astounding capacity for rationalization, especially when its structure of beliefs is in question. As strange as it may seem, it is not unthinkable to me that a person could stand with his hand on the body of a dead Sasquatch and still find some way to rationalize it away. These days, all it would take is someone to declare the dead Sasquatch "fake news" and no one would even look at it.

In the realm of spirit phenomena, I cannot think of anything that could possibly serve this function. The best we can hope for is audio, video, and meticulously documented field readings. But since all of these things are easily faked, none of it can be convincing when taken out of context.

Part of the issue is that as the technology for detecting more subtle phenomena advances, the technology for creating convincing hoaxes advances, too. Trying to prove the existence of the spirit world through technology is an exercise in chasing the horizon.

I have seen video footage and other evidence of Sasquatches from people whom I trust are not trying to hoax anything. I believe this evidence to be genuine. But I still cannot say that I am one hundred percent certain that Bigfoot exists. Isn't this a contradiction? The answer goes back to the dual mind model. At the objective level, I am completely convinced. I am apparently convinced enough to spend many nights through all four seasons in woods and swamps trying to find one. But my subjective mind is still using its escape hatch. While my objective mind fully accepts the validity of this evidence, it is still possible that it is faked or that it is a misidentification of some sort. There is still an escape hatch. So the subjective mind has no need to abandon its premise. Nothing has been shown to it that necessarily contradicts that premise.

This is why I believe that in the absence of personal experience, no secondhand report or evidence, no matter how compelling or how much you trust the person presenting it, can ever produce an RHE. This type of evidence only reaches the objective mind. It can never reach the subjective.

On the other side of the issue, I know plenty of people who trust me completely. I have no doubt of their faith that I would not hoax them or tell them anything that I believed to be even possibly mistaken. But when I show such people evidence we have captured on investigations, I am well aware it does not convince them that paranormal activity is real, at least not in the sense of producing an RHE and corresponding response. This is a large part of the reason that I am never in much of a hurry to show people evidence that I have captured over the years. If someone asks and is genuinely interested, I'm happy to share anything I have (unless it has been designated private by a client). But setting out on some sort of crusade to bring light to the masses is pointless. Rational argument will never cause the reaction that makes it real.

Paul: Interestingly enough, I think the role of evidence might produce the opposite effect regarding the existence of Sasquatch as opposed to the existence of ghosts or spirits. I'm not quite sure what would be considered evidence regarding the existence of ghosts. I think, though, that if the spirit of George Washington appeared and invited us to assemble *en masse* at the local mall so that he might have a conversation with us regarding the state of the country, the largest collective RHE ever would be the result. There also certainly would be panic on a global scale. If the existence of spirits, hauntings, and ghosts was proven beyond the shadow of a doubt, Pandora's box would open.

In regard to the Sasquatch phenomenon, however, while initially a finding would cause a lot of excitement, I think once the mystery was revealed, people would view Sasquatches in a more simple and clinical way. If a body was found and an autopsy and analysis performed, there would be less left to the imagination and the brain could therefore begin to formulate a match. If the doctors performed an autopsy on the body of a Sasquatch and came to the conclusion that it was simply a primate that somehow had gone undetected, and that the particular specimen tested suffered from a touch of gout and was a bit nearsighted, for many the Rabbit Hole Experience would be softened. Why? The subject would be classifiable. They could now make a correlation: a Sasquatch is simply an ape with a black belt in the art of hide-and-go-seek.

The most controversial contribution of evidence regarding Sasquatch has been the Patterson-Gimlin footage, shot in 1967 in the area of Bluff Creek in California. Proposed by some to be a smoking gun and by others to be nothing more than a guy in a suit, it has been analyzed, frame by frame, and discussed the world over. It's considered to be the most analyzed film in history with the exception of the footage of the JFK assassination. The anatomical proportions of the subject as well as its locomotion and appearance have been debated for decades.

Much like casts of footprints so detailed they show the surface ridges of the epidermis of the soles of the feet, I find the footage to be a prime example of evidence existing within a context. In my opinion, the footage is interesting for several reasons but mainly because of the muscle movement of Patty, the name given to the creature, which I feel would be difficult to duplicate with a limited budget in 1967. I also find the appearance of breasts on the creature interesting (get your mind out of the gutter), mainly because of the way the topic usually is discussed in the media, particularly at that time. Quite frankly, Bigfoot is always a "he." Rarely is the phenomenon portrayed as a population of animals with a male and a female in the mainstream media. Sasquatch is always "the big fella." I also think the appearance of breasts on a suit would be a much more difficult feat to authentically pull off.

That being said, the video is no smoking gun. Using the Patterson-Gimlin footage, though, I was able to duplicate—to an extent—a controlled RHE.

⊢——————————————————————

Case Study: Jim's Classification

Paul: In 2011 I struck up a casual conversation about the possible existence of Sasquatch with my friend Jim, who had no knowledge of the depth of my interest or the degree of time and money I've invested in investigating. I enjoy getting peoples' unbiased reaction to the topic, and have been guilty of introducing the topic in a casual manner among friends and acquaintances to gauge reaction. I truly am undercover.

"So what do you think of all that Bigfoot stuff?" I ask.

Jim was adamantly dismissive. When I'm engaged in these conversations, I merely suggest the possibility, which is consistent with my true feelings on the subject. When he cited a lack of evidence, I asked if he'd seen the Patterson-Gimlin footage. He hadn't and that didn't surprise me: he's almost twenty years younger than I am. I pulled up the footage on my computer and gave him a brief introduction regarding its history. Then I observed him as he watched.

It took approximately four seconds for Jim to exclaim, "That's not real!" I asked him to elaborate, and he couldn't. When I asked him how he came to the conclusion it wasn't real, his matter-of-fact response was, "Look at it." I obliged and replayed the footage.

"What confirms that it is not real?" I asked, genuinely curious as to how he arrived at his conclusion. He was insistent yet nonspecific.

"Just look at it," he repeated.

"I have looked at it," I said. "What observation brings you to the conclusion it's not real? Do you see a zipper? Perhaps a tag that reads 'dry clean only'? I'm fine with your assessment that the subject in the footage is not real, or at least not what is implied, but I'm interested in how you've arrived at that conclusion."

While he continued, unable to acknowledge any possibility that the footage may be authentic, his reaction grew stronger, more argumentative. His defenses became more intense. All he could say was, "Come on, man, look at it!"

He gave no definitive answer because he didn't have one.

This is a bright and articulate man I've known for years who is fully capable of communicating his thoughts and opinions. From the moment the footage started playing, his brain began interpreting what he was witnessing by using the catalog it has systematically built and maintained over his lifetime. When he exhausted the entire index of his mind and failed to identify the subject, he could draw only one conclusion.

"That's not real" is the other side of "I know what I saw." The former refuses the possibility; the latter insists on it. These reactions form the foundation of the cognitive dissonance that Michael outlined.

There was nothing definitive that led Jim to his conclusion. His brain threw up a question: *What the fuck is that?!*

For the sake of preserving sanity, the subsequent response was, "That's not real." Perhaps it is the brain's survival instinct to immediately slam shut the door of possibility.

While Jim kept repeating "That's not real," underneath the surface, I considered a different interpretation: "That better not be real!"

Michael: In this case, Jim's mind still had one possibility for a match—hoax. Many people take the approach that, as long as it's possible it's a hoax, it must be a hoax, regardless of how unlikely that is. This response allows a person to move forward with no consequences. When asked about the likelihood of the hoax possibility, skeptics (especially Skeptics) will say it's more likely a hoax than a Sasquatch.

But how do we know the probability of it being a Sasquatch? For Skeptics, Sasquatches don't exist, so the probability is zero. It keeps the math simple, anyway. Yes, zero is a lower probability than the probability of a hoax, even if that probability is .0001. But this is a bad way to test hypotheses.

The correct way is to begin by assuming there is no such thing as Sasquatch, and then asking: under this hypothesis, what is the probability of my experiencing what I am experiencing? If the probability is very small, then you must reject the hypothesis. The question becomes: what is the alternative hypothesis? Suppose Sasquatches do exist. Then maybe the probability of seeing one is far greater than the probability of a hoaxer pulling off the hoax of the century, or the half-century, as is the case with the Patterson-Gimlin film.

Suppose that instead of watching a video, Jim had walked into a Sasquatch while taking out the garbage. The mind goes through the same search of the catalog, coming up with no match, and would like to therefore say, "Not real." But this option is not on the table. A Sasquatch is standing there looking at him. What happens? Many times, the person will stand, their body frozen, their mind running through the catalog in a continuous loop. At the time, the mind cannot accept the option of "not real" or "misidentification" or "hallucination." But sometimes, after time and distance have elapsed, the person will be able to fall back on these options and avoid having to confront the other, scarier conclusion.

The Patterson-Gimlin footage offers a very interesting insight into how people react to what they cannot explain. Most people to whom I have mentioned the film believe it already was proven to be a hoax. I have not yet met someone who could identify a specific reference on the alleged proof: they just "heard about it one time." But this film has been around for fifty years as of this writing and it's still hotly debated. People are willing to write it off as a hoax using exactly the mechanism that Paul describes: they search their mental database for a match and come up with nothing, leaving them with the conclusion that it is fake.

I have always been on the fence about this film, as I am with just about any evidence I did not collect myself. When asked about it, I generally say that if it came out today, I would probably think it was a hoax but I just don't see how such a hoax could have been pulled off in 1967.

Recently, Bill Munns performed a great service to the Bigfoot community by producing a comprehensive analysis of the film in his book *When Roger Met Patty*.[15] Munns stays away from the controversies over the back stories of the people involved and claims of hoax and just sticks to an analysis of the film itself, which is really the only concrete piece of evidence we have. With his extensive experience in both Hollywood creature design and the technical aspects of film, he is a very capable person to conduct the analysis.

Munns examined every aspect of the film—from the creature itself to a frame by frame analysis of the shadows in the image and a retracing of the path that Roger Patterson ran as he filmed the footage. His conclusion is that nothing about the

---

[15] William Munns, *When Roger Met Patty: 1 Minute of Film, 47 Years of Controversy* (Charleston, SC: CreateSpace, 2014).

film is consistent with a hoax and that everything about it is consistent with a biological creature that was filmed spontaneously, just as Roger Patterson had described the situation.

Munns's book is dense, but it makes a compelling argument that, whatever the creature in the footage might be, the Patterson-Gimlin film is not a hoax. For me, the ball is now in the court of those who claim a hoax to contradict Munns's findings. So far I have not heard a single skeptic or hoax theorist address it. That's another indication of avoiding cognitive dissonance.

Nevertheless, it is still my contention that, by itself, no evidence can produce an RHE. I personally believe that the Patterson-Gimlin footage is authentic. But I still cannot say I am convinced of the existence of Bigfoot. My objective mind sees no way that the footage could be a hoax, but since I have still not seen the animal myself, my subjective mind has not been moved. Since it is still possible that it is a hoax, it does not have the RHE impact on me.

Paul: This discussion raises an interesting point regarding the perpetuation of hoaxes. While the purpose of this book is not to prove or disprove the existence of Sasquatch or paranormal activity, before one dismisses either as a hoax, one must consider the likelihood of a hoax versus the possibility of existence. When the details of a situation are examined, even if a hoax cannot be ruled out, one sees how the probability of a hoax is sometimes less likely than the probability of authenticity.

From a cryptozoological perspective, the concept that there is an undiscovered large bipedal creature living in the North American woods in the twenty-first century seems far-fetched. But weigh that against the likelihood that every single eyewitness account ever documented was a hoax or a misidentification. Which seems more likely?

Michael: While no amount of evidence can, by itself, produce an RHE, evidence can play an important role in the phenomenon. I have seen cases in which people who already have experienced phenomena with their own eyes and ears, and dealt with it, break down in tears when shown concrete evidence of the same phenomena. This occurs when people are in a state of dissonance after their experience but still hold onto their prior beliefs. They can doubt themselves and think that they imagined what happened or that they are going crazy. Once the evidence is in front of them, though, all of a sudden, the phenomenon is real to them. There is no turning back. The levee breaks.

Case Study: The Dancing Tripod

Michael: This case produced our most impressive piece of video evidence as of this writing. The footage was captured in a dance studio that we were called to investigate. Doors slammed in front of people. Objects moved. Apparitions were seen. So was a phantom black ball that bounced down a set of stairs and then vanished. There also was a very strange incident in which smoke apparently billowed from the mirrors during a class.

The client had called us because she was afraid her students were going to quit. Many had experienced these phenomena and there was a growing anxiety about the place. Many times, clients want us to find something to validate their own experiences. But this was a case in which the client was truly hoping we found nothing and that we could explain away the things that they were experiencing. We investigated and had a very quiet night. To be honest, when we left, we thought that we could pretty much explain all the claims in natural terms.

Then I reviewed the evidence. This is the difficult part of the job. Anyone can wander around a building at night, asking questions of ghosts and waving around fancy equipment. Afterward, though, come the seemingly endless hours of listening to audio of an empty room or watching video of the same scene for hours on end. On one occasion when I was reviewing video from our digital video recorder (DVR) system, which has no sound, the video hit the end of the recording. At that point, it pauses on whatever scene it happens to be showing at the time. I sat and watched the screen for another half hour before I even realized it had stopped. That's how dull most of the footage is. I often tell people that, like others, I go home at the end of the day and watch TV. But I watch the most boring programs on the planet.

The day after the dance studio investigation, I was watching the video from a camcorder I had mounted on a tripod covering a staircase where an apparition had been seen. I'd gotten home just before dawn and was dozing off as I watched. I was startled awake by a loud sound. I rewound the video. At one point, the camcorder view shook and there was a thud. It looked as if something had struck the camcorder. I thought perhaps a door had slammed or something had made it shake, so I reviewed the audio recordings. This confirmed that no one was in the building for at least fifteen minutes on either side of this event and no one had come in or out. The thud also seemed more faint on all of the audio recordings than it did on the camcorder, which led me to believe the sound was coming from the camera—not from something else that made the camera move.

This was interesting, but I would not be able to draw any conclusions without knowing what had hit the camera. Fortunately, we had several DVR cameras running that night in the same room where I had set up the tripod. I was hoping one of them could see what happened to the tripod. I called Todd, my team member, gave him the time stamp and asked him to check the DVR cameras, just for the hell of it. I did not expect to find anything. A few days later, he sent me a cryptic text: "We got it."

The Role of Evidence

There had been a DVR camera with a view of the tripod that filmed the entire incident. On camera, the whole tripod shifted on its own, all three legs sliding forward by several inches. Plain as day. We'd had DVR cameras filming that room from several angles at the time, so no one could come in or out without being on film. I was stunned. I was not stunned that such a thing would happen. I've seen objects move seemingly on their own on several occasions before and since. What stunned me was that we had it on film.

Consider that anything in that place could have moved and we would never have known about it. Even in this case, with no sound on the DVR the movement is so subtle that it would almost surely be missed. Instead, whatever or whoever was there chose to move the tripod that had a camera running on it. To me, this suggests that whatever it was wanted us to notice it. It seemed like a clear case of a spirit trying to get attention.

I knew that this footage was not going to be comforting to our client. She had called us in the hope that we'd be able to tell her nothing was going on. Instead, we were going to be telling her, "Yes, there appears to be some invisible entity present. And by the way, it can hit things and move them around if it wants to. Have a lovely evening." But our rule is always to provide our client with any evidence that we find.

As was our practice at the time, I sent out the final report with the clips to our team's founder, but I also explained I intended to drive the few hours to see the client personally to show her what we'd found. I wanted to be there to put things into context for her when she saw it, to ease her fall down the rabbit hole. Apparently something got lost in communication, and I found out the full report, including the video, had been sent to her.

I called the client as soon as I found out. I heard the fear in her voice. The video confirmed exactly what she'd been witnessing. It was all real. She was ready to pack up and look for a new profession. I tried to put things into context for her: we had captured absolutely no evidence of anything negative in the location, and we had no reason to believe she or her students were in any danger. Viewed in context, it seemed like whatever entity was present had specifically chosen to move something that we would be sure to see. The message seemed to be, "Hey, I am here!"

The vast majority of the times when we find evidence of some entity present, they seem to just be trying to get someone's attention. I explained to the dance studio director that many times, once they have gotten someone's attention, activity will calm down. They just want recognition. I told her we'd let things settle a bit and see how it went, while of course letting her know that if anything disturbing were to happen, we would be there for her.

A few weeks later we returned for a second investigation. This was both for our benefit (after all, we knew there was an active spirit present that wanted to communicate) and also to see how our client was faring. The answer was: not well. She was very distraught. She told us she was taking anti-anxiety medication and couldn't sleep. She had a severe case of Rabbit Hole Fever.

We decided to do some exposure therapy. We took her with us as we conducted our investigation to let her see there was nothing to fear. At one point, she felt something touch her arm. She broke down. We had to take her back to the office we were using as our base of operations. All the lights were on there. She was in tears and hyperventilating. She even left the building for a while. To her credit, though, she came back, seemed to have mellowed out a bit, and did another tour with us. We captured more good evidence on this investigation in the form of EVP, though nothing as dramatic as the video from the first trip.

We visited this location a few more times. Eventually, our repeated visits seemed to really help this client adjust to life in the rabbit hole. Not only did she learn to be comfortable working in one of the most active locations I've ever visited, she actually started to enjoy it. She would take her friends for little ghost hunting tours in the place and do EVP sessions, as we had shown her. There was no more talk of closing the studio.

Her attitude spilled over to her students. They took their cue from her and regarded the activity as something interesting and unique about the place. The ghosts were like their classmates. When we went back for a visit at a later time, some of the students asked us to sign autographs for them. It was very cute. I felt like we did some good and managed to catch some great evidence in the process. That is not a combination we find on every trip.

Michael: In this case, the evidence we captured during our investigation verified the client's experiences and sealed off the escape hatches. Until that time, she'd been able to rationalize what she was experiencing without taking the plunge down the rabbit hole. She was telling herself, *I'm not sure what I saw*. When she saw we had captured evidence of a seemingly impossible occurrence, just as she had described, the weight of all her own experiences could no longer be held up by the rational structures she had created.

This client's initial reaction to the evidence is one reason we do not encourage clients to investigate their own homes or place recorders or cameras around to film activity. I understand the temptation to do this to solve the conflict in the mind. But if they do catch something, they often are not prepared to handle the effects. Some clients know this. We often hear, "I want to know that what I am experiencing is real, but at the same time, I don't want to know." If that's not cognitive dissonance, I don't know what is.

Some investigators feel the same way. I hear many say they are fine going out to investigate other people's homes, but they will not investigate their own homes. They don't want to know. Most people need to have somewhere they can feel safe. Even if at some level they know nonphysical entities can go anywhere, as long as they don't have the evidence in front of them, they can tell themselves they are alone. Without realizing it, they are leaving themselves an escape hatch. If they were to see the evidence, that hatch would be sealed off.

The Role of Evidence

I have been asked an interesting question: if we knew this client would be terrified of the evidence, why didn't we just tell her we didn't find anything? After all, I have said that our goal is to put the client at ease.

There are a few answers for that. First, the client brought us in to investigate and show her what we found. That was the task we took on for her. Regardless of what we find, it is our responsibility to show it to her and give her our ideas about what's going on. If clients came to believe that we might not be telling them the whole truth after our investigations, then there would be little value in our work. It also would be patronizing to think that we should be the ones to decide who can handle the information and who cannot. That's not our call to make.

Second, although we might not believe there's anything negative or hostile at work, we could be wrong. I've been wrong before. Lots of times. After all, when we left the dance studio, we didn't think there was anything paranormal occurring at the location, but we were certainly wrong about that. It would be irresponsible for us to know a client is living or working in a building with spirits who have enough juice to move our equipment and not let her know.

On top of that, there's the issue that if the location is truly active, it is likely that the client is going to have that RHE at some point. It's better if we can guide her into it in a controlled way rather than leave her to face it alone later. It's like when you take fish and put them in a plastic bag in the tank so they get used to the water. Our role as investigators is to evaluate evidence from a bit of distance. If we catch something, we can look at it objectively, put it into context, and then interpret it for the client.

The Role of the Investigator

MICHAEL: Aside from collecting evidence and information, our second goal is to help the client or witness absorb their experience. We want to reduce any psychological conflict it may be causing and alleviate the fear and anxiety it can bring. In the end, that conflict is the reason witnesses contact us. They have experienced something that does not fit with their current belief system. They either want us to explain it so that it fits into their belief structure or prove to them their beliefs are incorrect and help them figure out where to draw new lines.

This process begins the first time we talk on the phone with witnesses. We assure them that we take them seriously and are there to help them. But we also try to keep the conversation light—not that difficult for us. These people have enough anxiety without us adding to it. My goal is to make the client feel better about their situation by the end of the first phone conversation.

For those witnesses who have gone too far to go back to their old beliefs, our most powerful tool to help them adjust to life in the rabbit hole is to take them with us during the investigation. Our approach here is very similar to the exposure therapy used to treat phobias. We take the client into the situation that causes them fear, under controlled conditions, in order to show them they can face their fears and deal with the situation. Participation allows them to see that we are not afraid of the activity, and that, unlike others to whom they may speak, we believe that such activity exists. Some of us have experienced it firsthand, but we are not afraid of it. That's precisely what these witnesses need to see.

In order for exposure therapy to be effective, it must take place in the same conditions that cause the person to feel fear. We are trying to communicate with the subjective mind, which responds to direct experience. If the client is terrified in the house at night, and we show up and do our investigation under the bright afternoon sun and then leave, the client is still going to be terrified once the sun goes down. We need to immerse the client in the same conditions in order to stimulate the subjective mind to create new premises. If we have a client terrified to be at home at noon, then we would do our investigation at noon. But due to the nature of fear, this is rarely the case. So the most effective time, from a therapeutic perspective, is in the darkest hours of night.

This assumes, of course, that we act in a way to alleviate the client's fear rather than augment it. We hear stories all the time of paranormal groups that go into a house, take the client into the dark, and then convince the client that there are demons and all kinds of things in the house. They attribute every noise to some malevolent spirit. Often, we are told, they hear a bang and proceed to pack up their gear and take off. This, too, is effective therapy — in the wrong direction. These teams are doing what they have seen on TV but without understanding why it's done. The teams on TV do not have clients with them. They are alone and trying to make things interesting for viewers who can turn off their TVs at the end of the show and go to bed in their safe homes.

We cannot behave that way when we have clients with us who are being influenced by our behavior. I don't care if a demon scratches you across the face and makes a clown doll bleed from its eyes, if you are with a client, you cannot show them your fear. (OK, if there's a clown doll involved, I might show some leniency.) Also, contrary to what some people seem to think, yelling and screaming and telling the spirits to "bring it on" is showing your fear!

Having the client present in a paranormal situation has the side benefit that it may help to stir up activity. If there is a person in the home who tends to experience most of the activity, then it makes sense for us to have the person with us. If I were a spirit at a location, and I saw a bunch of strange people running cameras and wires and carrying around a bunch of weird equipment, I would hole up somewhere and not make my presence known. We hope that by having the people who are normally in the home with us, it will break the ice and we are more likely to experience the activity that has been reported.

In the Sasquatch realm, Paul and I often take the same exposure therapy approach. True, we often go out into the field alone in the search for evidence. But in many cases, we are meeting with witnesses who've seen or heard something that terrified them. We will take these witnesses into the field at night in the location where they experienced the activity. We will show them how to knock on trees and make calls and look for evidence. They can see that we take this seriously but are not afraid. In fact, we are even hoping to find one of these giant monsters. In the same way as described in the tripod incident, if we can turn the witness's fear into curiosity, we can give them a much healthier way of dealing with their experiences.

On one occasion we camped out with a family of witnesses, complete with their dog, at a site where they reported having seen a family of Sasquatches walking along a dirt road. What an interesting investigation that turned out to be.

Case Study: The Dark Forest

Michael: In 2007 Paul and I met up with a family near the Catskill Mountains to investigate sightings they'd had in an area where they liked to camp. The place wasn't a formal campground—just a spot along a dirt road surrounded by woods that the father, Anthony, had hunted for years. The family reported that one day, they'd seen a family of hairy creatures walking upright along the dirt road there. Anthony's wife also claimed that later she witnessed something large walk through their camp at night while Anthony was sleeping.

We met with the family in the afternoon and explored the area with them to get a sense of the land while it was light. It was an interesting area featuring a network of trails and dirt roads. Along one of them, Paul and I found a pile of hundreds of pinecones that had been neatly and, clearly, intentionally stored. We considered that it might be people collecting them to use for crafts or some other use, but the place seemed like a long way off the beaten path to collect pinecones. We also found a very odd spot where the ground was soft and a whole row of full-sized trees had been partially uprooted so that they all leaned in the same direction and one rested on the next. I have never seen anything like it before or since.

Anthony also mentioned there were odd mounds with stones piled around them in one part of the woods. He gave us directions on how to find them but would not come along. Paul and I searched but never found them. It was late summer so the area was heavily over-grown.

As darkness approached, the family was getting ready to pull out, but we invited them to stay with us for the night. They had their boy with them as well as the family dog. Normally, we would not take along children or dogs when trying to be subtle and look for unknown creatures. But this was an area the family always had enjoyed for camping and they seemed too disturbed to stay there. We wanted to alleviate their discomfort. We also thought that having them there for the night might shed more light on what actually had occurred.

We all pitched tents and got a campfire going. The family pitched theirs near the cars. I planted mine farther back in the woods, hoping to catch something off guard. As we sat around the fire that night, we chatted with the family. Coyotes howled. I noted there was one call among them that seemed off.

The family seemed relatively comfortable but not eager to wander far from the fire. Imagine their dismay around midnight when Paul and I announced we were going for a stroll along the dirt roads. It was about as dark along those roads as I have ever experienced. Paul and I were walking only a few feet apart, but I would never have known he was there had I not been able to hear him. We could make out the dirt road only by a very subtle difference in the shade of black under our feet. These were the days before I owned a thermal imager. I had a primitive Russian army surplus digital night vision device, but looking into it rendered me blind for several minutes afterward, so I used it sparingly.

The Role of the Investigator

As we walked along the road, we heard something rustling in the brush next to us. We stopped. As we stood in the absolute darkness, we heard what sounded like footsteps running toward us: the sound came from the woods and approached the road we were on until it stopped mere feet from us. I turned my night vision on the area and looked all over but could not find anything that would make the sound. I did not say a word, as I did not want to influence Paul. But I didn't have to.

"That sounded small, didn't it?" he said. I agreed. It certainly did not sound like a giant primate, but it didn't sound like something as small as a squirrel, either. To me, it sounded more like the footsteps of a child. Then Paul noted the second thing I was thinking. "But it sounded like it was on two legs, didn't it?" Again, I had to agree.

It was a very strange experience. I could not see any animals around that would make such a sound. After the sound stopped, it never started up again. Whatever had made the sound should have still been right in front of us.

We had another odd experience the next day after our family of witnesses had left for home. Paul and I stayed around and wanted to make another try at finding the mysterious mounds Anthony had mentioned. We'd wandered the woods for an hour when we came upon a section so dark and dense, it seemed to come straight out of the Brothers Grimm. The trees were packed tightly and beyond the first line of trees, there was absolute blackness. A thin fog hung over the dark forest. This was on a bright, sunny day in August.

The Rabbit Hole Experience

Paul and I looked at each other, silently wondering which of us was going in. Paul volunteered. I had visions of him being cooked up in a gingerbread house, but we decided I would stay on the perimeter and maybe we could flush something out. As he wandered through the forest of darkness, I walked the outside. At one point, one of us must have spooked something because I heard something take off and run, crashing through the trees. I tried to get a look at what it was, but the forest was so thick, I couldn't see anything. It sounded large, though, and made a hell of a racket breaking branches as it ran. I didn't think it could possibly have been a deer since they move gracefully through the woods.

We never did get to see any large primates on the trip. But it was a very strange area and we had no trouble believing something odd was going on there. A year later, I made a trip back to the spot and camped for a couple of nights on my own. I still was not able to find the mounds, and some development had started making its way up the dirt roads. Within a few years, the area would likely have a neighborhood built on it. The Department of Environmental Conservation had put up a "No Camping" sign on a tree next to where I camped (I didn't see it until I was leaving, I swear!). I also heard a lot of gunplay during the day and, upon investigation, found a firing range had been set up nearby. I don't think any hairy primate in his right mind would have been residing in the area. But as for less material creatures, who knows?

Paul: In the Sasquatch field, it's the need for resolution that motivates people who've had these experiences to reach out to us. My main focus is to investigate the Sasquatch phenomenon and draw conclusions that ultimately lead to answers, but one of my most important functions is to ease the witness across the aforementioned line. After the initial experience has jarred their perception of reality, they need validation. They need someone to confirm that they are not crazy and not alone in their experience. I can't help but laugh when so many witnesses preface their account to me with "I know this sounds nuts, but—"

Consider they're speaking with a grown man who has spent countless hours roaming the wilderness in the dead of night hitting trees with baseball bats and whooping with his ghost-hunting amigo. Any concerns regarding my judgment are unfounded, to say the least.

In regard to the Rabbit Hole Experience, once they have landed on the other side of the line, I can welcome them with a martini and a plate of hors d'oeuvres, suggest they take a few deep breaths, and assure them everything is going to be alright.

Often they provide me with the details of their experience. Then we spend an extended period of time talking about Sasquatch and cryptozoology. Here's where I hope to allay fears that often are unrealistic but always understandable. I introduce the concept of Bigfoot as an animal. Although an extremely unique animal, to say the least, Bigfoots have a lot in common with other animals, including ourselves. They require food and shelter for survival and are extremely shy for obvious reasons.

For a long time, when media outlets approached the topic of Sasquatch, they did so tongue in cheek, with few exceptions: "And tonight Wink Winkleman reporting on the Bigfoot craze. The big fella was seen up in Burlington, Vermont, and then somehow must have jumped down to the outskirts of Atlantic City, New Jersey. How does he do it? Film at eleven."

Bigfoot has long been portrayed as one being with an implied ability to appear and reappear hundreds of miles away. Often Sasquatches have been reduced to the same level at which one would consider unicorns and leprechauns. With respect to both, I've yet to meet anyone who could look me in the eye with a straight face and make a serious claim to have seen either.

To my knowledge, there are no casts.

Only recently has the possibility of a yet-to-be discovered flesh and blood hominid, established by a breeding male and female of a population that contains both old and young, been discussed with any consistency. In regard to the Rabbit Hole Experience, this is where the violent collision of reality versus the unreal starts. When one believes to have experienced a subject long portrayed as either the result of superstition, infantile and wishful thinking, or a monster, there will be psychological consequences.

The Role of the Investigator

Michael: Most people are introduced to the spirit field by watching *Ghost Hunters*, or, in less fortunate cases, some of the other TV ghost hunting shows. In many of these shows, the so-called investigation team wanders around an old building — or, worse, someone's home — yelling and screaming at unseen entities to come out and take them on. Then they play some audio clips that might possibly be interpreted as something that might sound vaguely similar to a human voice. Maybe they show some video clips of so-called orbs accosting them in various places. Then they declare the location haunted, congratulate each other on their bravery, and move on to the next location.

People watching these shows get the impression that this is what paranormal investigation is about. As a result, we get a lot of calls from terrified homeowners who have called in some local group to investigate their claims of activity. The group behaved as seen on TV, yelling and trying to pick a fight with what might well be the family's late grandmother. Then they heard a noise, perhaps the heater kicking on, declared the house to be under demonic control, and beat a hasty retreat, leaving the family so terrified that they spent the rest of a sleepless night preparing their house for the market. Generally, the family will never hear from the group again. After all, this is where the investigation, if you want to call it that, ends on TV.

The Rabbit Hole Experience

When I go into an investigation with my team, I see our job as a form of social work with the possibility there may be paranormal activity involved. That mindset even affects how I choose which cases we will investigate. After interviewing a potential client, my criterion is not whether I expect to find paranormal activity at the client's house. It is whether I feel that by going there, we can leave the clients with more peace of mind than they had when they called. We often investigate cases where I honestly don't expect to find anything paranormal, though sometimes we are surprised.

The truth of the matter is that, even in cases where there's legitimate activity, the probability of us being able to find solid evidence of it in a limited period of time is very low. We do our best. On occasion we do find evidence to confirm what the clients are experiencing. But we are very aware of the one key problem with our work: If we go into a location and find solid evidence, that gives us information about what is taking place. If we go into a location and find no evidence, that doesn't mean there's no paranormal activity taking place. It just means nothing took place near one of our cameras or recorders while we were there. At the end of the investigation, we can only say that we have no information either way.

We also come at the problem from the opposite angle and investigate possible natural explanations for what the client is experiencing. Then we put the two together to try to figure out the most likely explanation for the clients' experiences. If there are reasonably likely natural explanations, and we find no paranormal evidence that cannot be explained in this way, then it is likely that the phenomena do not result from paranormal causes. Unlike many skeptics, however, we always recognize that we can never say for sure.

In the meantime, we help clients figure out what they've experienced and how to deal with it. In some cases, that may mean explaining that not everything that goes bump in the night is paranormal. Some clients find that a great relief. They did not like the shady look of that white rabbit, anyway. Other clients will insist that what they experienced was paranormal even if we find that very unlikely. Since it is always possible we missed something, we will then treat the client as having had a paranormal experience. Since that is their perception, there is no reason to debate the point. In many of these cases, however, I get the impression that the client's objective mind is fully convinced they had a paranormal experience though their subjective mind is not buying it.

The relatively rare case is one in which the client has had a genuine, bona fide, certified RHE. Generally, it is fairly clear in talking with these clients that they are staring into the abyss. You can see the look in their eyes. Unlike those discussed above, in many cases these people are still unsure in their objective mind about what actually happened. They may still be trying to come up with rational—that is, natural—explanations. But their subjective mind will have none of it.

They say, "I still can't believe it, but I know what I saw." In these cases, we still go about the usual business of collecting evidence, but our main job is to help this person realize they can still go on. Cognitive dissonance has a social component. Part of the discomfort comes from having beliefs that are in conflict with those of the people around you. By letting them know there are people who believe the paranormal to be real, the discomfort is immediately reduced.

I always carry with me the memory of an astoundingly cold weekend when I first met the TAPS team at the Otesaga Resort Hotel in Cooperstown, New York. I will never forget how liberating it felt to openly converse with people who know these things are real and yet do not let the knowledge keep them from enjoying life and having a good time. Shortly afterward, I joined Scientific Paranormal, the TAPS Family team that I now run, to help others achieve that same feeling.

I try to take this feeling with me to every home that we investigate. I assure the client that we believe them and that we will do everything we can to help them. We are not going to walk out the door and disappear, leaving them on their own. At the same time, I will make jokes to the client about the activity. My approach is to take the client seriously, take the work seriously, but not take the paranormal too seriously.

My team and I have fun during investigations. That's more than appropriate. It's essential. It is not because we view our investigations as something fun to do on a weekend night. Our attitude is a very intentional choice. The client needs to be shown that what has happened is not the end of the world. It does not (usually) mean they are under attack by evil forces. It means their world has expanded.

I tell my team that if we go into a location acting frightened and very serious, the client will believe things are serious and that they should be frightened. If we go in acting like these things happen but they're not that big a deal, then the client will see what's happening through the same lens. Achieving the balance is difficult. We have to make sure the client realizes we are taking their situation and claims seriously. If there are children involved, we need to convey to the client that our primary goal is making sure there is no threat to the children. But my team has a very strong record. Generally speaking, by the time we leave the location, the whole atmosphere of the place has changed. The clients are joking along with us, feeling more like this is something they can handle, and knowing that if they cannot handle it, we are a phone call away. This is the state the clients should be in if we're doing our job. If the clients are more frightened when a team leaves a house than when they arrived, the team should have stayed home and watched ghost shows on TV.

In many cases, I just discuss a situation with a client by phone and that is enough. Oddly, not everybody wants a bunch of people wandering around their house in the wee hours of the morning trying to talk to ghosts. Or in some cases, an investigation may not be possible for other reasons. Often, just having someone listen to their story and not think they're crazy is enough to put them more at ease.

Case Study: Kevin's Kitchen

Paul: I experienced the exact scenario Mike just outlined—not as an investigator with the BFRO but as a close friend of a man who was having potentially paranormal experiences.

Kevin, like a lot of friends of mine, had no knowledge of my role as a BFRO investigator. We'd worked together for the same biotech company, shared a love of sports, and became friends over the years. We hadn't seen each other for quite a while and met up for dinner one evening to catch up. We met at a local Italian restaurant and shot the breeze over dinner. I motioned for the waitress and requested the check. As we waited for her to return, I asked Kevin if he wouldn't mind going for a walk around town. It had served as my old stomping grounds some twenty-five years earlier.

The Role of the Investigator

"Sounds good, man," he said. "There is something that I'd like to talk to you about." I saw the seriousness in his eyes and sensed it in his voice. Kevin launched into the typical preface that Mike and I hear so often. "I know you're gonna think I'm crazy, but—"

As I opened the door and we spilled onto the road, my heart sank. Kevin was like a younger brother to me and had been through a lot at that time in his life. I didn't like to consider the possibility all was not well.

He proceeded to tell me what was wrong in that all too familiar rapid-fire manner so many witnesses use. It's as if they feel they'd better hurry up and get it all out before they change their minds. Or perhaps they've internalized their experience so long that when they release their pent-up anxiety, they lose control and their words are like a swollen river over a dam.

"I've been having some weird shit going on, man. I've been having this thing where I wake up and I, I can't move. I'm like … paralyzed."

"Hmm." I nodded calmly. "How long has that been going on?"

"A few times over the last few months," he said. His eyes were wide, and as we walked side by side, he continued talking. All the time, he was looking straight ahead. I wonder if he avoided eye contact for fear of feeling judged. Or perhaps it was easier for him if he continued talking without the distraction of someone looking at him. Perhaps the reminder that he was actually relaying such an experience to another human being would have made it too difficult.

"I wake up, and I can't move, man," he went on. "I know I'm not dreaming. I'm wide awake. And the last time it happened, I felt like someone was holding me down." I was silent, allowing him to contribute more detail and suppressing the urge to fill in the blanks for him.

"I've also had this thing where, uh, I wake up, and I'm like—" He licked his lips nervously. "I'm like floating over my body." Behind my calm demeanor and my encouraging nod were two unspoken words: *Holy shit.*

Kevin proceeded to tell me another experience he'd had a few months earlier in which he stopped at his mother's house on his way home from work. Finding no one in the house, he decided he would grab a quick shower while he waited for her to return. Later he was adamant about the fact he was in the shower no more than ten minutes. He had a few things that he wanted to accomplish that evening and was conscious of the time. He quickly got dressed and returned to the kitchen no more than fifteen minutes later. Upon entering the kitchen, he said, he saw that every single cabinet and drawer was wide open.

"Every cabinet was wide open—every cabinet," he said. "You know the two cabinets that everyone has over their fridge where you put the shitty liquor that no one ever drinks, and they get sealed shut because you never open them? Even those cabinets were wide open. And that's not all." I looked at him with eyebrows raised, waiting for the conclusion.

"The contents of the cabinets were neatly stacked in the center of the kitchen floor," he said. "Cereal boxes, silverware, pot holders, dish towels, all placed very systematically in the middle of the kitchen floor. Not dumped, but placed."

While Kevin was in the kitchen trying desperately to make sense of it all, his sister had returned home from shopping. He asked the question he knew he had to ask even though he had the answer. His sister and mother had both been out all day. Their father was working. The kitchen was untouched before Kevin entered the bathroom to take a shower. Interestingly enough, Kevin and I share one of many obsessive-compulsive traits upon both leaving and entering our homes: we lock the door.

In the fifteen minutes that it took Kevin to shower, get dressed and return to the kitchen, had someone compromised one of the locks, broken into the house, opened every kitchen cabinet and drawer, stacked the contents neatly on the kitchen floor, and exited the house undetected?

Or was there some other explanation?

Kevin and I had leaned on each other while we went through our respective hard times. We shared a similar sense of humor and were close enough that we could talk to each other about anything without fear of judgment or ridicule. I chose not to tell him about my research as a Sasquatch investigator for the same reason I chose not to tell the overwhelming majority of my friends and family. I simply failed to see any reason to tell them.

Not knowing what else to do, Kevin could come up with only one response: he called the police. To their credit, the police took the report seriously, investigated, had no conceivable explanation, and left. By process of elimination, their explanation was that someone was responsible.

On the surface, the experience Kevin had in the kitchen is not necessarily linked to the more recent out-of-body and paralysis experiences he was having. But the point was that his sense of reality had been challenged, and, for his mental health, he needed someone to help him reestablish the line between the real and the unreal.

By sheer coincidence, I knew just the person that he should speak to. I explained to Kevin I would call a close friend who investigated potential paranormal activity. I told Kevin I'd relay the details of the experience and then touch base with him regarding Mike's feedback. I knew ultimately they would need to have a direct conversation in order for there to be true progress. But baby steps were in order.

As I knew would be the case, Mike didn't bat an eye. I may as well have been discussing the details of the sandwich I had for lunch. Mike was matter of fact about Kevin's experience, but that wasn't all.

"I've had that experience," he said. I should've known.

After a few days to allow Kevin's experience to sink in, I called him and relayed some of my conversations with Mike. I stressed that it would be best for him to reach out directly to Mike for a conversation. After the expected hesitancy on his part, and the subsequent reassurance on mine, Kevin and Mike had a series of conversations regarding his experiences. After quite a few weeks had passed without Kevin mentioning any disturbing experiences, I thought it safe to inquire.

"So the situation that you've been discussing with Mike, where are you with that?" I asked. "Everything OK?"

"Oh, yeah," he said. "Thanks a lot for referring me to Mike. He helped me gain a whole new perspective on it. The last few times it happened, I just kinda went with it. I just figured the hell with it—I guess I'll just float around the room."

Mike had ushered Kevin across the threshold and accompanied him into the rabbit hole. The details of Kevin's experience hadn't changed, but, thanks to Mike, his perception of them had. He experienced a paradigm shift.

I talked in detail with both Mike and Kevin regarding their conversations, as I was interested in how they reached their conclusion. Since Michael is much more qualified, I'll ask him to elaborate on what was discussed and how Kevin's interpretation of his experiences changed from paralyzing fear to *The hell with it—I guess I'll just float around the room.*

Well done, Professor. Float on, Kevin.

Michael: Kevin had been dealing with stressful family issues, and it seemed as though activity would pick up when he was under stress. What finally got him to call me was that he'd been lying in bed one night and reported that something had grabbed his ankles and pulled him halfway down the bed. He said he could feel the hands on his ankles. This had only happened one time, but often he reported having a feeling as if there were someone in the room with him.

We are always concerned when activity turns violent or negative (though many times, clients interpret it as negative when that may not be the case), so my initial questioning centered around the incident of being grabbed and pulled in bed. I wanted to know how certain he was that he had been awake during this incident, and that it had not been a dream.

I asked whether he'd had to pull himself back up on the bed to where he was before he was yanked: if he had, that would require awareness. He said he did recall shuffling himself back up. Still, it's always difficult with reports of activities that happen while the person is in bed, since it often can be unclear where the line between dream and real experience may fall.

Apart from this episode, Kevin's experiences of waking up and being paralyzed could be attributed to the phenomenon of sleep paralysis that should be well known to paranormal investigators. The body paralyzes itself in REM sleep (the level of sleep in which dreams occur) as a defense mechanism against the person hurting himself while dreaming. Sometimes, a person can wake up while this paralysis is still active. Awakening in such a state can be very frightening to the person, and since their brain is still partly in sleep mode, they may interpret the experience in all sorts of ways, sometimes even combining the experience with hallucinations. Under stressful conditions such as Kevin's, more severe reactions are common.

If these had been the only reports, I might have been inclined to attribute the experiences to these natural causes. But other parts of the activity seemed less easily attributed to dreaming. For instance, the cupboards had opened and all their contents had been stacked on the floor when Kevin was fully awake, unless the police were part of his dream as well. The fact that there were external phenomena occurring suggested to me that something of a paranormal nature might be involved. The stressful conditions Kevin had been experiencing made me consider the possibility of a parasitic entity. Such beings feed on negative energy and so activity will increase when the host is under stress or depression. They also can do things to try to keep the person in that distressing state since it keeps their food supply running.

Over the years, it has become my opinion that parasitic entities are at work in many cases where demonic activity is suspected. But parasites generally don't make a habit of big displays that would draw attention to themselves. Stacking all the contents of the kitchen cupboards in the middle of the floor sounded more like classic poltergeist activity, and there are many in the paranormal field, including me, who believe that poltergeist activity is generally caused unconsciously by a person involved.

Kevin also described having experiences in which he would find himself apparently outside of his physical body while fully conscious. This terrified him and he would panic, thinking he might be dead and unable to get back into his body. He told me about this very hesitantly, as if he were expecting me to ask him to stay on the phone while I called a tailor I knew who could extend the sleeves of his jacket for him. Instead, he was surprised when I responded that I had experienced the same thing many times. When I said this, I felt the tension on the phone suddenly lift. He was relating to me things he'd experienced that made him feel isolated and possibly crazy. I explained to him that it is likely that people do this all the time but just don't remember it. The conversation really loosened up at this point, and he began to talk about many things he'd been experiencing.

As Kevin went on with his tale, a hypothesis began to take shape. The fact that he was having and recalling out-of-body experiences (OBEs) suggested he probably was doing this frequently and not remembering it most of the time. This probably was the cause of his feeling that there was someone in the room. It is a relatively common occurrence that a person will project their etheric double, often called the astral body, and then wake up in their physical body while the double is still out. The result is that the person is paralyzed, though awake, and when the etheric double comes back into the room to reunite with the physical body, the person experiences its presence as the feeling there is an entity in the room, though it's actually just a part of himself. This is a well-known phenomenon among occultists but seems to be less recognized among paranormal investigators. Many cases of spirit activity as well as, perhaps, some reports of aliens entering a person's room at night may be attributable to this phenomenon. I suspected that this might be what Kevin was experiencing.

Kevin's frequent OBEs suggested that he seemed to have some talent at projecting parts of his etheric substance. Frederic Myers refers to this trait as psychorrhagic diathesis[16] and suggests that it may explain cases where a person is seen in more than one location at the same time, a phenomenon known as bilocation. To understand how this could cause physical phenomena, it is useful to add Carl Jung's concept of autonomous complexes.[17] These are splinters of the subconscious psyche that split off from the main conscious personality and essentially act outside of the control of the person. In dramatic cases, they can manifest as multiple per-

[16] Myers, 196.

[17] C.G. Jung, *Collected Works of C.G. Jung*, vol. 8. *Structure and Dynamics of the Psyche* (Princeton: Princeton University Press, 1970), paragraphs 194–219.

sonality disorder, but often they act in a more sub-tle way, causing the person to occasionally act in ways that seem inconsistent with, or even directly contradictory to, the person's normal personality. Kevin told me that he was obsessive-compulsive and would never leave drawers and cupboards open, but that made what happened all the more compatible with this explanation. The fact that the incident occurred at his mother's house, the scene of a lot of his current stress, also fits in with this theory.

Combining these elements, a possible explana-tion for the incident is that Kevin had formed an autonomous complex due to his current stress. His tendency for psychorrhagic diathesis then may have created a vehicle for this splinter of his per-sonality to manifest and it lashed out in the kitchen, emptying cupboards and drawers while he was physically in the shower. This may be the mecha-nism of a lot of poltergeist activity. To be clear, this does not necessarily mean that if you were in the kitchen, you would have seen the items float into the center of the room. A very common report in poltergeist cases is that activity occurs seemingly in an instant as soon as witnesses turn their backs. So, the kitchen floor could be clean, a person standing there turns his back for a second and when he turns back to the kitchen, all of the contents of the cup-boards are stacked on the floor. And the whole thing happened silently. How this happens is a question well beyond the scope of this book, but such things are reported fairly frequently in poltergeist cases.

Of course, this is all just speculation, but as far as I could tell, the only real sign of any external entity being present was the report of being pulled down the bed. This is difficult to judge. Often, when a person is projecting out of their body, they experience feelings as if their physical body is moving, though it is really the etheric double that is moving. This was why I asked Kevin whether he had to pull himself physically back up on the bed. He said that he did but he did not seem too sure how far down he had moved. It's possible that he had not really moved at all and that his mind had just interpreted the experience that way.

Of course, there is always the possibility that Kevin was actually being victimized by some parasitic entity, even a demonic one, but without doing an investigation, I did not hear anything that necessarily suggested that to be the case.

At first Kevin had a hard time wrapping his head around the idea that he might be the cause of what he was experiencing. He asked me a lot of questions about whether such things are possible, and all I could tell him was that in my experience, it seemed that they were. As the conversation went on, he seemed to get more interested in this idea and its possibilities.

"So does that mean I can move things with my mind?" he asked. I laughed.

"Well, maybe so, but unfortunately it's the sub-conscious mind that controls it," I replied. "You are probably not going to be able to clean out Atlantic City any time soon. The good news is that if you're aware of this and can work on reducing your stress a bit, you can probably prevent big piles of kitchen supplies on the floor."

As for the OBEs, I explained to him they are a perfectly natural thing and probably were due to his stress levels. When he was under stress, his sleep was disrupted and he would wake up during the episodes. I told him that when it happened, he should consider it an opportunity to see where he could go and what he could do: Try flying around the house. Try going outside. I also told him to try pushing his body through a closed door or win-dow. I love doing that. It is such a weird feeling, like you're squeezing through a sieve. Well worth the price of admission.

I believe two aspects of our conversation changed the way Kevin looked at his situation. First, he found that he was not alone in these expe-riences, that other people had them and he was normal in this sense. The reassurance immediately reduced the dissonance he was feeling. He could possibly have thought I was patronizing him, ex-cept that at several points, I asked questions that anticipated events that he had not yet relayed to me.

"Wow, it's funny you mention that," he would say, realizing I was speaking from experience.

Second, when I suggested that Kevin himself might be the cause of the activity, his attitude switched from fear to something akin to curiosity. This was a possibility that was completely new to him and something he wanted to consider. It also seemed to be a possibility that did not cause as much conflict in his mind.

When activity such as this occurs, people tend to feel like they're under attack. In some instances, that may be the case, and certainly I want to know if that is true. But in many cases, it is not. For Kevin, considering that he might be the cause of his experiences, and that they might be revealing a whole new world of possibilities for him, caused a huge shift in the way he viewed his situation. Moving from fear to curiosity is a powerful way to change a person's attitude.

When I spoke to Paul later, after he had talked to Kevin again, he said Kevin seemed a whole lot more relaxed. He was still having OBEs but now considered them kind of cool. He was trying to work with them. He had not experienced any more phenomena such as being grabbed and pulled. It sounds like he may have tendencies that will make it difficult for him to ignore the rabbit hole, though when his stress eases up a bit, activity will likely calm down.

The main thing is, he's not scared of what's happening anymore, and even recognizes he has a new aspect of life to explore.

Paul: I'm jealous and feel left out. I wish that I could just "float around the room."

Michael: You'll get your chance. No need to rush it.

V. Living with the Rabbit

MICHAEL: While putting the finishing touches on this book, I began having issues at my cabin. On several evenings, I returned home from work to find lights on in the house. At first, I assumed I'd just neglected to turn them off before I left, but as mentioned earlier, I am not a big fan of lights in the best of times. After several such incidents, I began suspecting something else may be going on.

So I initiated a routine. Before leaving the house, I would systematically check to make sure everything was off. Then, to make my point, before I walked out the door, I would stand in my living room and announce out loud that I knew everything was off. So if I came home and found a light on, I would know there was something out of the ordinary happening.

I did this every day, and over the next week or so I had several occasions on which I came home and found lights on again. One day it was the kitchen, another day the bathroom. Then, one night I went out for the evening about 7 o'clock. I stood in the dark before I left and announced that everything was off. When I got home three hours later, one of my oil lamps was burning brightly.

Although I'd had several similar experiences since the original candle incident, I'd never been as systematic about checking everything as I was during this period in time. There always had been the possibility, however small, that I had simply left a lamp burning. In this case, there could be no mistake, though. I had verified that everything was off before I left. The game was up.

Great. So what now?

On a macro scale, this is where the field of paranormal investigation seems to be today. *Ghost Hunters* aired its last episode a few days before Halloween 2016, and the timing seems to be fitting. Paranormal investigation existed long before this show, of course, and will exist for a long time to come, but this was the show that really ushered in the era of investigators attempting to prove the existence of paranormal phenomena by capturing evidence using modern technology. That era now seems to be coming to a close.

That's not to say everyone in the world is completely convinced of the reality of the spirit world, or that the question of an afterlife has been resolved beyond dispute. There are some Skeptics who will never be convinced, and this is fine, but it is time to accept that gathering further evidence in an attempt to convince such people is fruitless. Parapsychologist and statistics professor Jessica Utts[18] has made a telling observation about research into psi, a parapsychological term for experiences or phenomena, including telepathy and telekinesis, that can't be explained by materialist science. She writes scientific evidence for psi effects is far stronger than that showing aspirin helps prevent heart attacks. For anyone who takes a genuine scientific look at the evidence, the existence of paranormal phenomena has been proven, statistically speaking, for a long time. For those who still question this evidence, more of the same is not going to change anything.

I am sympathetic to the skeptical position. I read and listen to skeptical analysts and generally find myself in agreement with their conclusions about the most likely explanations for particular cases. I just don't generalize this to mean that the phenomena don't exist. My personal experiences will not allow this. In the absence of personal experience, the skeptical stance is probably the one that makes the most sense. Its only flaw is that, at least in the case of spirit activity, it happens to be wrong.

[18] Jessica Utts, "The significance of statistics in mind-matter research," *Journal of Scientific Exploration 13*, no. 4(1999): 615-38.

There are others who accept the evidence and are convinced at the objective level of the reality of the spirit world, but not at the subjective level. I have argued in this book that no amount of second-hand evidence can create the RHE and reach the subjective level of the mind, so in this sense also, the added value of another video, EVP, or even double-blind scientific experiment is minimal.

This leaves those who have had direct personal Rabbit Hole Experiences, for whom there was no need for any other evidence to begin with. At this stage, the value in any more TV shows with people wandering around buildings at night trying to prove that a place is haunted seems very limited, except for pure entertainment purposes.

We are now left with a different set of questions. Assuming that we accept ghosts and spirits are real, that paranormal phenomena and nonhuman contact do occur, what now? What does this mean for us as human beings? What do we do with this information? How do we move forward?

Despite the domino effect this knowledge can have on a person's psyche, accepting the reality of spirit phenomena does not necessarily require a person to drastically change their life. As author, blogger, and chaos magician Gordon White[19] has

---

[19] Gordon is the author of the *Rune Soup* blog, https://runesoup.com, and of several books, which are included in our bibliography. The quotation is from an

said, "Just because sharks exist doesn't mean everyone should become a marine biologist, but anyone can still get eaten by a shark." Or, for that matter, a rabbit. These experiences will continue to happen to people, just as they always have. Perhaps it's time we recognize that the solution to our collective cognitive dissonance may be to stop falsely invoking science in trying to convince people of the unreality of experiences that humans have had since there were humans.

On a personal level, my team and I will continue to investigate individual cases. The purpose of these investigations for me was never really to gather evidence for the sake of proving the existence of paranormal phenomena to others, but rather to try to determine what was going on and why so that we could help the client resolve the situation, fit this new information into a reshaped belief structure, and move forward in life. That task will always be relevant.

This is not to say there is nothing further to be learned from investigation. The gathering of information can still serve to increase our knowledge base about how the world works. But it is now a process of rabbit hole cartography rather than discovery. For example, on two separate cases in a recent year we had the experience of hearing and recording clear footsteps on the floor above us

interview with Greg Carlwood on the Higherside Chats podcast (plus version) posted September 13, 2016.

while we were on the ground floor of a building. Meanwhile, recorders in the room above, where the footsteps seemingly originated, did not capture the sounds. How are we to make sense of this phenomenon? What might it tell us about the nature of the nonphysical world, and how might we use this to interpret experiences at other locations?

On a broader scale, we should shift the focus of our questioning from whether paranormal phenomena are real to what it means for us that they are. If spirits are around, how do we relate to them? What are our responsibilities to them? Our ecosystem has gotten larger, maybe infinitely so, and we need to reorient our place in it.

Then of course there is the Big Question. One of the most fundamental questions of being human is whether our consciousness continues to exist after physical death. For those who truly fall down the rabbit hole from the spirit side, that question has been answered. And there is no way to view life the same way once that knowledge is digested.

Fortunately, we are not learning something new but relearning something we have only recently forgotten. Modern Western culture is dominated by the paradigm of scientific materialism, the idea that only things that we can physically measure are real and therefore the only valid objects for scientific inquiry. But this view is a relatively recent and isolated phenomenon in human experience. Civilizations all over the world and throughout history have recognized forces and beings that exist outside of the material world, and considered them just as real as anything that could be seen and touched. This is not because they were superstitious primitives, but because the RHE has been a part of human experience since the beginning. There is nothing unscientific about wanting to study these phenomena. In fact, to those who have experienced them, the outright denial of their existence is the attitude that is unscientific. Scientific materialism has served a purpose, but it is time for us to learn to use the two words separately. Once you have visited the rabbit hole, using them together causes cognitive dissonance.

Paul: I've investigated the Sasquatch phenomenon for well over twelve years. Since 2005 countless footprints have been cast, thousands of photos have been introduced, and hundreds of videos have been debated. Yet none of what most people would consider definitive proof has been introduced into the discussion. As far as the mainstream world is concerned, the argument for the existence of a yet-to-be-discovered primate roaming the woods of North America has not been advanced.

I must agree. But that doesn't affect my belief in Sasquatch. It only means that proof beyond a reasonable doubt has yet to be provided.

Does the accumulation of additional circumstantial evidence tip the scale? Whether we have one hundred casts of footprints, or one million, does it matter? Whether we have a few blurry pictures of what some allege to be a Sasquatch, or a few thousand, does it make a difference?

My personal opinion: it doesn't.

Sure, it's exciting for those of us who have been on the front lines. Any time someone comes across a fresh footprint, and the end result is a cast that shows definitive features that both share similarities with and yet are significantly different from those of a human, it reinforces the possibility for me personally. Anytime someone introduces a video or photo that is not easily reconciled, it opens the door. Yet the general public is disinterested: "Oh, look. Another blurry photo that's supposed to be Bigfoot." They roll their eyes. In this day and age of cyber smoke and mirrors, photos and videos simply cannot be authenticated with 100 percent certainty.

Hell, we've been debating the Patterson footage for fifty years. At this point only DNA will do and that can only mean one thing: a body, dead or alive.

I wouldn't consider anyone shooting a Sasquatch in order to produce the smoking gun to be a hero. The idea of killing an individual to solve the mystery is a self-serving one. It's not worth it to me. Perhaps a hiker will come across the body of an individual who has died from natural causes, but I know how unlikely that is.

Living with the Rabbit

I've roamed the woods ever since I could walk, and with the exception of animals that have been hit by cars, the number of carcasses that I've found is statistically low when compared to the amount of time I've spent in the forest. The decomposition process is a rapid one. Mother Nature is efficient.

But what if we found a Sasquatch? What if one were captured alive?

The thought of an animal—believed by many to be a close relative of ours—in a cage, being poked and prodded is not an attractive one. Then what do we do? Release her back into the wild with an identification tag tattooed on her arm? A radio transmitter collar around his neck so we can track his every move? Do we log onto our Facebook pages so we can watch the Sasquatch Cam?

Would the spectacle to inevitably follow compromise what could be an Earth-shattering scientific discovery?

Would the woods be overrun with new curiosity seekers who know Sasquatches exist and just want a selfie with one? Recently I was on social media watching video of a group of seals being harassed by such curiosity seekers. In this particular case, curiosity seekers would be defined as Facebookers with cell phones so drunk on their own self-indulgence that they are oblivious to the impact of their behavior on animals they obviously appreciate.

The Rabbit Hole Experience

People with the best of intentions can inflict incredible damage.

I was in the swamp in southwest Florida on a beautiful nature preserve I often frequented when thirty feet ahead of me on the path one day was a couple in their mid to late twenties. She was standing behind him, obviously afraid of something. He was in front of her with an eight-foot tree branch in his hand. As I made my way toward them, he turned to me.

"Cottonmouth," he said. I looked to my right, and there she was. I wasn't surprised. She was always there—beautiful and wild, coiled up on a rotting log. In fact, if I were a Cottonmouth, I couldn't think of a nicer section of swamp for an afternoon nap.

As the man lifted the branch toward my cold-blooded friend, his female companion, the voice of reason, simply said, "Don't. Leave it alone." Good advice. Cottonmouths are ornery.

"I'm not going to hurt it," he replied. "I just want to see what it does."

He couldn't contain the six-year-old within him. He had to pick up a stick and poke the snake, just to see it react. He had to elicit a response. At best the cottonmouth is denied a few moments' peace. At worst our curiosity seeker gets bitten and goes to the hospital. Or perhaps it's the other way around. Maybe at best he goes to the hospital.

Living with the Rabbit

Life isn't easy for a cottonmouth or a Sasquatch and that's the mentality I fear in the event we let the Bigfoot out of the bag, so to speak.

I'm also interested in the impact a newly discovered North American primate would have on conservation efforts, and curious as to the subsequent political ramifications. When old growth forests in the Pacific Northwest were depleted by the timber industry in the 1990s, the population of Northern Spotted Owls there plummeted. Environmentalists and animal rights activists petitioned the U.S. Fish and Wildlife Service to classify the owl as an endangered species. The request sparked debate about the impact such a move could have on the local economy: the loss of tens of thousands of jobs, resulting in bankruptcy, foreclosure, and starvation for many. Such battles continue to be waged all over the globe.

I live just north of the border of the Pine Barrens, a tract of wilderness that exceeds a million acres across southern New Jersey and is home to our very own Jersey Devil. Over the years, both road and home construction have been halted due to the presence of the endangered timber rattlesnake as developers and conservationists battle the issue in court.

If an owl and snake can pose that kind of division, the discovery of a species that so closely resembles our own surely would have mind-blowing significance on the land use debate. It may be difficult to convince some that we have to set habitat aside for a snake, but when it comes to our hairy, bipedal cousins, even the most hardened business-man would be forced to consider the impact of construction upon our newfound friends. Would people be willing to sacrifice the potential econom-ic gains? Call it mammalian chauvinism, but I know guys who have no problem catching, gutting, and eating fish but who can't bring themselves to hunt bear. Why? They're too much like us.

If Sasquatches are found, federal and state gov-ernments would face tremendous challenges for which they are ill prepared. Could this be reason enough for the government to discourage the re-lease of evidence supporting their existence?

They've eluded us for a long time, and with good reason. If they are here, they have survived without our help. They certainly don't need us.

From time to time I think of Allen, recalling his experience of watching a hairy, bipedal creature while he was out on his property in the Adirondack Mountains. I hear his voice in my head: *They're probably better off without us.*

Maybe one day some witnesses will be vindicat-ed by the discovery. They can say to their families, friends, and neighbors, "I told you so." Others such as Allen will continue to be indifferent, simply grateful for the experience. Some will suppress their experiences in the dark corners of their minds.

Living with the Rabbit

Mike and I will continue to seek our own answers, and our seeking will inspire more questions. We have set up shop in the rabbit hole. We've kicked off our snake-proof boots and hung a few pictures on the wall. Frozen pizzas are in the oven, and Mike's phantom roommates have lit candles for ambiance. We live in the rabbit hole, and we will be here to welcome you should you ever find your way down.

Acknowledgments

MUCH thanks to the Bigfoot Field Researchers Organization for the education that I've had the privilege to receive. Most of you I've never met, but I'm truly grateful.

Thanks to Lorraine and Bill for their support and input.

To all those who investigate the unknown, risking their reputations, putting their preconceived ideas aside, opening to possibility, and putting the truth above all, despite the consequences.

And to whoever lit the candle that night Mike and I returned to the cabin—nice touch.

Honorable mention to Amy's® Organic Frozen Pizza and Califia Farms® Triple Espresso, for one gets hungry in The Hole and must be razor-sharp.

—Paul Conroy

My deepest gratitude goes to my Scientific Paranormal New York team—Catherine, Todd, Diane, Pat, Leeann, Hayley, Chris, and Dawn of the Dead.

When I'm in a dark building with a demon in the closet, I want them there with me.

Special thanks to Catherine for taking me on-board and to Adam, who founded the group.

Thanks also to the great people on our Connecticut team and others we've worked with over the years.

I am grateful to The Atlantic Paranormal Society (TAPS) for supporting us and entrusting us to investigate their cases and assist their clients and to all the clients and witnesses who took us into their homes and woods. I hope we were able to do some good.

Many thanks to Lorraine and Bill for seeing promise in this project and for all the help in making it manifest.

Thanks to Deonna for her invaluable help with the book and her friendship.

Deep gratitude to Huck for belaying me on a particularly dark excursion down the hole and considering that the bizarre shit I was telling him might actually be real.

And to Ashley, who met me at a fork in my road and steered me onto the road less traveled by. It has made all the difference.

Lastly, I acknowledge she who led me down the hole initially and showed me that my ideas of what was possible were far too narrow.

—Michael Robartes

Bibliography

Bartholomew, Paul, Robert Bartholomew, William Brann, and Bruce Hallenbeck. *Monsters of the Northwoods*. Utica, NY: North Country Books, Inc., 1992.

Bartholomew, Robert E., and Paul B. Bartholomew. *Bigfoot Encounters in New York and New England: Documented Evidence, Stranger than Fiction*. Blaine, WA: Hancock House, 2008.

Festinger, Leon. *A Theory of Cognitive Dissonance*. Stanford, CA: Stanford University Press, 1957.

Festinger, Leon, Henry Riecken, and Stanley Schachter, *When Prophecy Fails: A Social and Psychological Study of a Modern Group That Predicted the Destruction of the World*. New York: Harper Torchbooks, 1956.

Holzer, Hans, *The Ghost Hunter's Strangest Cases*. New York: Fall River Press, 2006.

Hudson, Thomas Jay. *The Law of Psychic Phenomena: A Working Hypothesis for the Study of Hypnotism, Spiritism, Mental Therapeutics, Etc.* Chicago: A.C. McClurg and Co., 1896.

Jung, C.G. *Collected Works of C.G. Jung, Vol. 8: Structure and Dynamics of the Psyche*. Princeton: Princeton University Press, 1970.

Kelly, Edward F., Emily Williams Kelly, Adam Crabtree, Alan Gauld, Michael Grosso, and Bruce Greyson. *Irreducible Mind: Toward a Psychology for the 21st Century*. Lanham, MD: Rowman & Littlefield, 2009.

Munns, William, *When Roger Met Patty: 1 Minute of Film, 47 Years of Controversy*. Charleston, SC: CreateSpace, 2014.

Myers, Frederic W.H. *Human Personality and Its Survival of Bodily Death*. New York: Longmans, Green, 1907.

PTSD Alliance. "What is PTSD or Posttraumatic Stress Disorder?" http://www.ptsdalliance.org/about-ptsd (accessed June 2017).

Radford, Benjamin. *Scientific Paranormal Investigation: How to Solve Unexplained Mysteries*. Corrales, NM: Rhombus Publishing, 2010.

Utts, Jessica. "The significance of statistics in mind-matter research." *Journal of Scientific Exploration* 13, no. 4 (1999): 615-38.

Bibliography

Vallée, Jacques. *Anatomy of a Phenomenon: Uniden tified Objects in Space — A Scientific Appraisal.* Chicago: Henry Regnery, 1965.

White, Gordon. *Pieces of Eight: Chaos Magic Essays and Enchantments.* 2016.

———. *Star.Ships: A Prehistory of the Spirits.* London: Scarlet Imprint, 2016.

———. *The Chaos Protocols: Magical Techniques for Navigating the New Economic Reality.* Woodbury, MN: Llewellyn Publications, 2016.

About the Authors

Michael Robartes

Michael Robartes leads Scientific Paranormal, a paranormal investigation team in The Atlantic Paranormal Society (TAPS) Family network. A lifelong explorer of unexplained phenomena, he knows what eyewitnesses go through and helps them integrate their experiences into their worldview. Robartes lives in New York State.

Thermal image confirming the presence of Michael Robartes at a recent night investigation.

Paul Conroy

Paul Conroy conducts investigations for the Bigfoot Field Researchers Organization (BFRO). He has studied the Sasquatch phenomenon from the

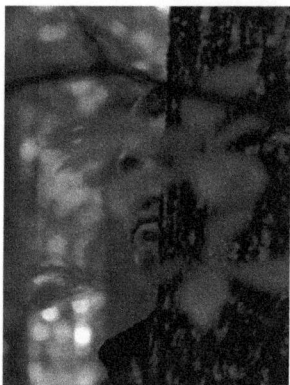

Everglades to the Canadian border for thirteen years. When not pursuing the unknown, he roams the wilds, practices martial arts, reads, and writes. Conroy and his furry four-legged daughter Koda live in the Jersey swamp.

A sighting of the elusive Paul Conroy in the New Jersey woodlands.

Learn more

For additional information about Paul Conroy, Michael Robartes, and *The Rabbit Hole Experience*, including events with the authors and contact information, visit the Rabbit Hole Experience website at **www.rabbitholeexperience.com.**